A NEW THEORY OF URBAN DESIGN

A New Theory of Urban Design is the sixth in a series of books which describe an entirely new attitude to architecture and planning. The books are intended to provide a complete working alternative to our present ideas about architecture, building, and planning—an alternative which will, we hope, gradually replace current ideas and practices.

volume 1   THE TIMELESS WAY OF BUILDING

volume 2   A PATTERN LANGUAGE

volume 3   THE OREGON EXPERIMENT

volume 4   THE PRODUCTION OF HOUSES

volume 5   THE LINZ CAFÉ/DAS LINZ CAFÉ

volume 6   A NEW THEORY OF URBAN DESIGN

A NEW THEORY
OF
URBAN DESIGN

Christopher Alexander
Hajo Neis
Artemis Anninou
Ingrid King

New York • Oxford
OXFORD UNIVERSITY PRESS
1987

Oxford University Press

Oxford   New York   Toronto
Delhi   Bombay   Calcutta   Madras   Karachi
Petaling Jaya   Singapore   Hong Kong   Tokyo
Nairobi   Dar es Salaam   Cape Town
Melbourne   Auckland

and associated companies in
Beirut   Berlin   Ibadan   Nicosia

Copyright © 1987 by The Center for Environmental Structure

Published by Oxford University Press, Inc.,
200 Madison Avenue, New York, New York 10016

Oxford is a registered trademark of Oxford University Press

Library of Congress Cataloging-in-Publication Data

Alexander, Christopher.
A new theory of urban design.
Bibliography: p.
Includes index.
1. City planning—Philosophy.   2. City planning—
California—San Francisco—Simulation methods.
I. Neis, Hansjoachim.   II. Anninou, Artemis.
III. King, Ingrid.   IV. Title.
NA9031.A38   1986   711'.4'01   85-25854
ISBN 0-19-503753-7

2 4 6 8 10 9 7 5 3 1

Printed in the United States of America
on acid-free paper

CONTENTS

INTRODUCTION   1

PART I. THEORY   7
1. *The Idea of a Growing Whole*   9
2. *The Overriding Rule*   17
3. *The Seven Detailed Rules of Growth*   31

PART II. EXPERIMENT   101

PART III. EVALUATION   233

ACKNOWLEDGMENTS   251

A NEW THEORY OF URBAN DESIGN

INTRODUCTION

In this book we describe an experiment which we did in 1978. The experiment was extensive, and involved a large number of people, over a long period of time.

When it was finished we decided that we must write it up. It seemed too important to leave unpublished.

At the same time, it was very hard to describe exactly what we had achieved. We had a manuscript which described the experiment. But even the manuscript left it unclear just what we had achieved. During the last six years, we have come back to the manuscript from time to time, trying to decide how to describe the work we did in this experiment.

Finally, after considering many possible interpretations of what we had done, we realized that what we had was, quite simply, a new theory of urban design. This isn't something we set out to create. And there is a danger that the title might seem pretentious—because what we have is very incomplete.

On the other hand, "A new theory of urban design" really does describe what we have. We have a formulation of an entirely new way of looking at urban design, together with a detailed experiment which shows, in part, what this new theory can do. The fact that the theory is—so far—still full of holes, and incomplete, doesn't alter the fact that it is, in principle, an entirely new theory. And so, for this reason, we have let the title stand.

When we look at the most beautiful towns and cities of the past, we are always impressed by a feeling that they are somehow organic.

This feeling of "organicness," is not a vague feeling of relationship with biological forms. It is not an analogy. It is instead, an accurate vision of a specific structural quality which these old towns had . . . and have. Namely: Each of these towns grew as a whole, under its own laws of wholeness . . . and we can feel this wholeness, not only at the largest scale, but in every detail: in the restaurants, in the sidewalks, in the houses, shops, markets, roads, parks, gardens and walls. Even in the balconies and ornaments.

This quality does not exist in towns being built today. And indeed, this quality *could* not exist, at present, because there isn't any discipline which actively sets out to create it. Neither architecture, nor urban design, nor city planning take the creation of this kind of wholeness as their task. So of course it doesn't exist. It does not exist, because it is not being attempted.

There is no discipline which could create it, because there isn't, really, any discipline which has yet *tried* to do it.

City planning definitely does not try to create wholeness. It is merely preoccupied with implementation of certain ordinances. Architecture is too much preoccupied with problems of individual buildings. And urban design has a sense of dilettantism: as if the problem could be solved on a visual level, as an aesthetic matter. However, at least the phrase "urban design" does somehow conjure up the sense of the city as a complex thing which must be dealt with in three dimensions, not two.

We have therefore used the phrase urban design in the title of this book, since it seems to us that urban design, of all existing disciplines, is the one which comes closest to accepting responsibility for the city's wholeness.

But we propose a discipline of urban design which is different, entirely, from the one known today. We believe that the task of creating wholeness in the city can only be dealt with as a *process*. It cannot be solved by design alone, but only when the process by which the city gets its form is fundamentally changed.

Thus, in our view, it is the *process* above all which is responsible for wholeness . . . not merely the form. If we create a suitable *process* there is some hope that the city might become whole once again. If we do not change the process, there is no hope at all.

This book is a first step in defining such a process.

3

The process we define, is rooted in a sequence of earlier theoretical and practical innovations.

During the early 1970s a group of us succeeded in isolating a large number of so-called "patterns," which specify some of the spatial relations necessary to wholeness in the city. The patterns we defined ranged from the largest urban scale to the smallest scale of building construction. The patterns themselves have been published and discussed in volumes 1 and 2 of this series.

In volume 3, *The Oregon Experiment*, the authors showed that a complete and implementable planning process, based on these patterns, could allow the users of a community to take charge of their own environment, and that people could channel the process of development into a healthier course, by using these patterns.

The work reported in volumes 4 and 5 later showed that the physical geometry of an architecture based on these patterns would be entirely different from the one we know, and also that, to produce it, the process of building production would have to be changed drastically.

And other even more important discoveries were being made. During the period of 1976–1978 one of the authors (CA), had become aware of a deeper level of structure lying "behind" the patterns. At this level of structure it was possible to define a small number of geometric properties which seemed to be responsible for wholeness in space. Even more remarkable, it was possible to define a single process, loosely then called "the centering process," which was capable of producing this wholeness (with its fifteen or so geometric properties) at any scale at all, irrespective of the particular functional order required by the particularities of a given scale.

Thus, the centering process seemed capable of generating wholeness in a painting, in a tile, in a doorway, in the plan of a building, in the three-dimensional constellation of spaces which form a building, in a garden or a street, even in a neighborhood.

So far, the theory of these spatial properties and of the centering process, remains unpublished. It will appear in a later volume of this series, "The Nature of Order."

However, as a result of these discoveries, two of the authors (CA and IK) began, in the early part of 1978, to imagine an entirely new kind of urban process, that was guided in its entirety by this single "centering" process.

More exactly, we began to imagine a process of urban growth, or urban design, that would create wholeness in the city, almost spontaneously, from the actions of the members of the community . . . provided that every decision, at every instant, was guided by the centering process.

We decided to test this idea by performing an experiment.

We first postulated a series of seven rules, to embody the process of centering at a practical level, consistent with the real demands of urban development.

We then took a part of the San Francisco waterfront (about thirty acres intended for development in the near future) and simulated an imaginary process which makes use of these seven rules, to govern all development over a five-year period.

The result of this simulation are described in Part two of the book.

Within the simulation, it is possible to see a new part of the city growing under the influence of our seven rules . . . and finally we see the end result of this process, as it might have been after a period of five years.

The experiment is partially successful. Although it lacks many important details, and although many practical matters remain to be worked out, nevertheless, in broad outline it does work.

It creates wholeness—or some approximation of it—in a way which is entirely different from the way that urban planning and design work today. And it does also seem to have the *potential* for creating wholeness far more deeply than was possible in our simple experiment.

We believe that it presents the beginning of a new theory for the three-dimensional formation of cities.

PART ONE

THEORY

CHAPTER I

THE IDEA OF
A GROWING WHOLE

When we say that something grows as a whole, we mean that its own wholeness is the birthplace, the origin, and the continuous creator of its ongoing growth. That its new growth emerges from the specific, peculiar structural nature of its past. That it is an autonomous whole, whose internal laws, and whose emergence, govern its continuation, govern what emerges next.

We feel this quality very strongly, in the towns which we experience as organic. To some degree we may know it as a fact about their history. To some degree we can simply feel it in the present structure, as a residue.

This kind of growing wholeness is not merely something that existed in old towns. It exists, always, in all growing

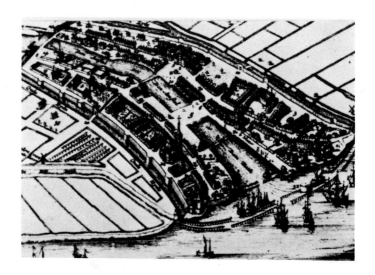

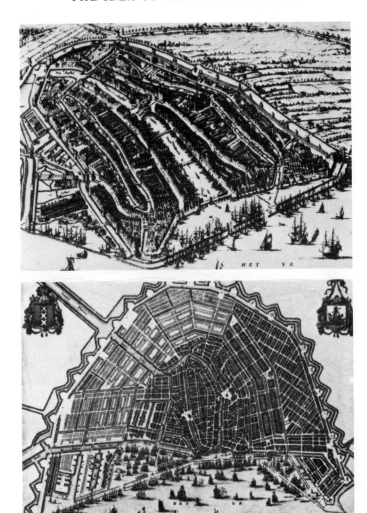

The growth of Amsterdam

11

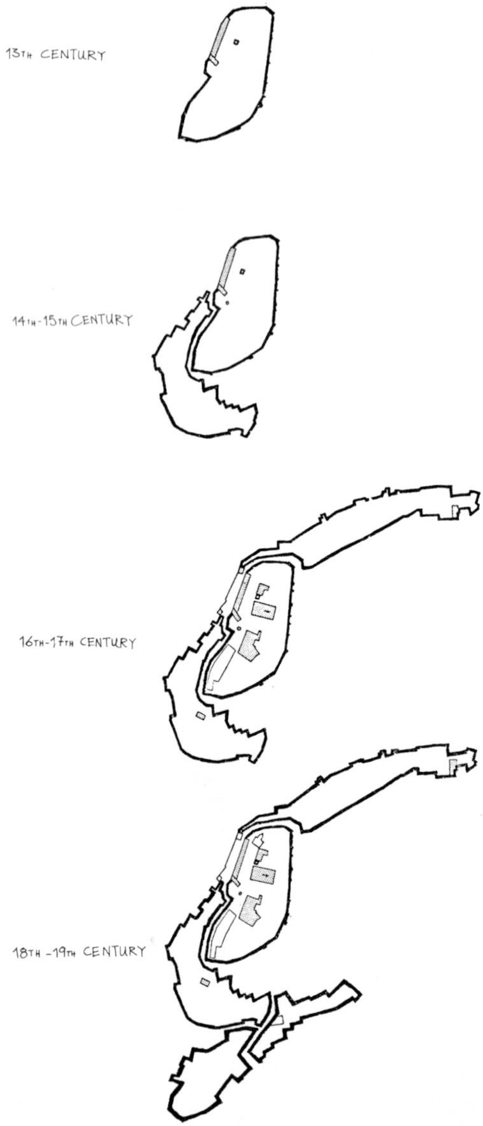

13TH CENTURY

14TH-15TH CENTURY

16TH-17TH CENTURY

18TH-19TH CENTURY

Growth of a hill town

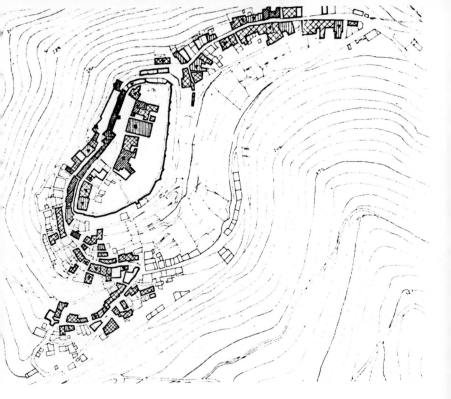

organisms (which is why we feel that old towns are somehow organic . . . simply because they share, with organisms, this self-determined, inward-governed, growing
wholeness). And it exists, also, in all great works of art. It
exists in a good painting, during the time of its creation. It
exists in a poem.

In each case, we are aware that the future growth of the
thing is created, from the present, by an impulse towards
wholeness. Somehow, this impulse towards wholeness is allowed to govern the next steps in the creation, the expan-
sion, the formation of details . . . the formation of the
largest and the smallest wholes.

13

This feature exists, also, in a dream, whose evolution is again governed by the history of where it has been so far. And it exists in a children's bedtime story, made up as we go along. Each sentence, coupled with the child's delight, tells us what fantastic thing will happen next, inspires us to fill out the fantasy, to bring it back upon itself, again to make it whole.

∿ ✦ ∿

In each of these growing wholes, there are certain fundamental and essential features.

First, the whole grows piecemeal, bit by bit.

Second, the whole is unpredictable. When it starts coming into being, it is not yet clear how it will continue, or where it will end, because only the interaction of the growth, with the whole's own laws, can suggest its continuation and its end.

Third, the whole is coherent. It is truly whole, not fragmented, and its parts are also whole, related like the parts of a dream to one another, in surprising and complex ways.

Fourth, the whole is full of feeling, always. This happens because the wholeness itself touches us, reaches the deepest levels in us, has the power to move us, to bring us to tears, to make us happy.

All traditional towns have these features in their growth.

But the modern practice of urban development does not have these features. It does not deal with growing wholes at all.

First, although the growth often is piecemeal, the piecemeal character does not contribute to a growing wholeness. It is merely piecemeal, and produces unrelated acts, which lead to chaos.

Second, the growth is not, in any deep sense, unpredictable. It tends, most often, to be controlled by conceptions, plans, maps and schemes. But these plans do not have the capacity to generate a growing wholeness. Instead they force an artificial, contrived kind of wholeness.

Third, planned development is also generally not coherent . . . not in a deep-felt sense. It is supposed to be. But if we ask ourselves whether the final product of current urban design projects actually is coherent in the real, deep sense that we know from traditional towns, then we must say no. The order is superficial, skin deep, only in the plan or in some contrived orderliness of the arrangements. There is no deep inner coherence, which can be felt in every doorway, every step, and every street.

And fourth, this modern planned development which we think of as normal, certainly has NO power to evoke deep feeling. It can, at best, ask for some kind of admiration for "design." But of deep feeling there is no word, not a tremor, not a possibility.

∾ ✤ ∾

Let us ask, then, what kind of process might actually be capable of giving wholeness, true wholeness, to a town.

According to the summary of wholeness we have given, it is clear that the wholeness will have to come from the *process*. And, concretely, the process will have to guarantee

15

that each new act of construction becomes related in a deep way, to what has gone before.

This can only be accomplished by a process which has the creation of wholeness as its overriding purpose, and in which every increment of construction, no matter how small, is devoted to this purpose.

Such a process can exist.

In the text which follows, we shall outline—tentatively—the nature of an experimental process which is capable of producing wholeness dynamically, in this fashion, and will then give rules for such a process. The rules are detailed enough to become operational in a city.

In Part two, we shall show, by means of a simulated example for the San Francisco waterfront, how the process works in practice.

In Part three we shall evaluate the results of our experiment, and summarize the nature of the process once again.

CHAPTER 2

THE OVERRIDING RULE

Let us consider what kind of process might be needed to let a city become gradually whole.

In nature, the inner laws which make a growing whole are, of course, profound and intricate. In many cases, as for instance in the case of a poem forming in a person's mind, or in a painting which forms itself, we never ask ourselves what these laws are . . . there is no need to . . . it is enough, for one person, unconsciously, to allow it to occur.

In the case of biological organisms, we have begun to ask ourselves more concretely what these laws are. But the history of biology in the last fifty years—the period when this question has been seriously asked—only makes it clear how immensely difficult a question it is. Although we know that such laws must be there, concretely, at every level from the genetic, to the cytological, to the global, our capacity to understand, and describe these laws in a coherent enough way to account, properly, for the growth, the development, the morphology of the emerging organisms, is still incredibly small. Said quite simply, we do not know how it works. The chances are that we shall be able to describe it properly, at some time in the next hundred years.

With a city, we don't have the luxury of either of these cases. We don't have the luxury of a single artist whose unconscious process will produce wholeness spontaneously, without having to understand it—there are simply too many people involved. And we don't have the luxury of the patient biologist, who may still have to wait a few more decades to overcome his ignorance.

What happens in the city, *happens to us*. If the process

fails to produce wholeness, we suffer right away. So, somehow, we must overcome our ignorance, and learn to understand the city as a product of a huge network of processes, and learn just what features might make the cooperation of these processes produce a whole.

We must therefore learn to understand the laws which produce wholeness in the city. Since thousands of people must cooperate to produce even a small part of a city, wholeness in the city will only be created to the extent that we can make these laws explicit, and can then introduce them, openly, explicitly, into the normal process of urban development.

We are faced then, with the question: what kinds of laws, at how many different levels, are needed, to create a growing whole in a city or a part of a city.

As we shall see in the document which follows, even in this "rough draft" of a process we have found it necessary to define a surprisingly rich and complex system of laws (or rules), which operate on seven different aspects of structure. A large part of the text which follows, will be devoted to our efforts to make clear the ways that these seven rules operate.

However, before we begin our discussion of the different laws, or rules, operating at their different levels, we must first develop a clear sense of their general purpose.

We do this by formulating a single, overriding rule, which governs all the others.

/ Let us consider a town, or a part of a town, which is growing and changing.

And let us imagine, now, a single process which exists, throughout this town, at many levels. We place the emphasis on the word *single*. The process is a *single* process because it has only one aim: quite simply, to produce wholeness, everywhere. /

⌈ Of course, in detail, the growth of a town is made up of many processes—processes of construction of new buildings, architectural competitions, developers trying to make a living, people building additions to their houses, gardening, industrial production, the activities of the department of public works, street cleaning and maintenance, and so on and so on. /

But these many activities are confusing and hard to integrate, because they are not only different in their concrete aspects—they are also guided by entirely different motives.

The welfare department is trying to build houses at low cost to help poor families. The department of transportation is trying to speed up traffic flow in the city. City officials are concerned with keeping disparate functions separate by means of the zoning ordinance. The officials behind the counter are trying to follow rules strictly so that they will not lose their jobs. Houseowners are trying to keep their houses in good order. Landlords are trying to make as much money as possible from their rents, and to spend as little as possible to get it. Sierra Club members are trying to make sure that nature is respected in the city.

Many of these aims are valuable and good within themselves.

But since they are so disparate, it makes it very hard to see what overall aim the growth of the city is really trying to accomplish. One gets confused by the multiplicity of aims, and then, ultimately, the overall growth and construction of the city is not guided by any clear motives— only by a hodgepodge of these many different motives.

Of course, one might say that this hodgepodge is highly democratic, and that it is precisely this hodgepodge which most beautifully reflects the richness and multiplicity of human aspirations.

{ But the trouble is, that within this view, there is no sense of balance, no reasonable way of deciding how much weight to give the different aims within the hodgepodge./

For example, within the view current in the 1970s and 1980s, transportation has become immensely powerful. Indeed, transportation requirements have achieved an entirely *unreasonable* level of power over the decisions which are made in the city.

In this case, the hodgepodge is not neutral or democratic at all. And this is typical. Some things get overemphasized. Others get underemphasized. Altogether there is no sense of the *whole*. The famous hodgepodge simply creates such a mental confusion, that various particular human goals, can suddenly become powerful, and others fall into oblivion, almost by accident, and our cities are then shaped by an unbalanced system of pressures, which—far too often— leaves essential considerations out of the picture altogether.

For this reason, we propose to begin entirely differently. We propose to imagine a *single* process . . . one which works at many levels, in many different ways . . . but still essentially a *single* process, in virtue of the fact that it has a *single* goal. And what is this single goal: simply, the creation of wholeness in the environment.

This is not as naive as it sounds. In fact it is helpful, because—although wholeness is hard to define, and can evoke so many discussions—still, most people have a rather good intuitive sense of what it means. It is, therefore, a very useful kind of inner voice, which forces people to pay attention to the balance between different goals, and to put things together in a balanced fashion.

Our single overriding rule, may thus be formulated as follows:

Every increment of construction must be made in such a way as to heal the city.

In this sentence the word "heal" must be understood in its old sense of "make whole." It includes not only the repair of existing wholes which are there already, but also the creation of new wholes.

We consider the fabric of the city, at any given point, healed or not healed, to the extent that it is composed of a series of interconnected, overlapping wholes. In the course of the next 200 pages, the definition of "a whole," and "healing" will become clear by example.

Most simply put, the one rule is this:

Every new act of construction has just one basic obligation: it must create a continuous structure of wholes around itself.

In "The Nature of Order," a manuscript first drafted in 1978, but still unpublished, a series of key results are presented on the nature of wholeness.

22

These results establish the following facts:

1. Wholeness, or coherence, is an objective condition of spatial configurations, which occurs to a greater or lesser degree in any given part of space, and can be measured.

2. The structure which produces wholeness, is always specific to its circumstances, and therefore never has exactly the same form twice.

3. The condition of wholeness is always produced by the same, well-defined process. This process works incrementally, by gradually producing a structure defined as "the field of centers," in space.

4. The field of centers is produced by the incremental creation of centers, one by one, under a very special condition. Namely:

As one center X is produced, so, simultaneously, other centers must also be produced, at three well-defined levels:

a. Larger than X. At least one other center must be produced at a scale larger than X, and in such a way that X is part of this larger center, and helps to support it.

b. The same size as X. Other centers must be produced at the same size as X, and adjacent to X, so that there is no "negative space" left near X.

c. Smaller than X. Still other centers must be produced at a scale smaller than X, and in such a way that they help to support the existence of X.

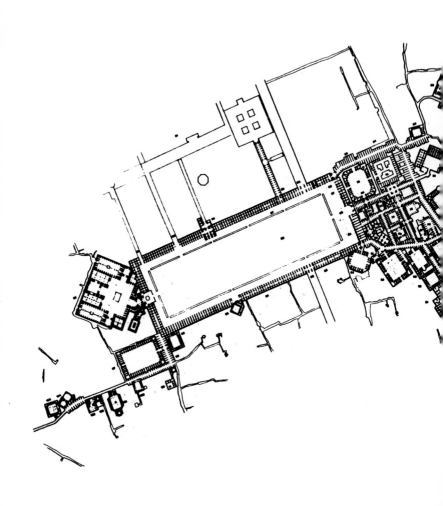

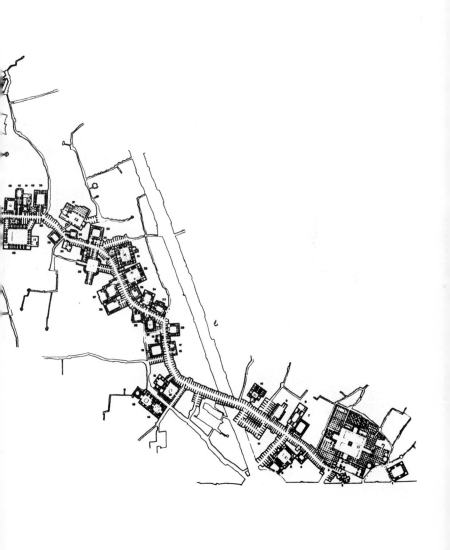

This process is hard to grasp. It is hard to grasp, partly because the concept of a center itself is not easily defined, and can only be defined recursively. This means, that even *understanding* of the concept of the center can only be achieved gradually/

The process itself also has many subtleties and complications. The few lines on page 23 only represent a mechanical version of something which is far deeper, when correctly understood, and never mechanical.

And yet, if this "one rule" is to be applied in practice, it cannot be obscure.

[In a city, where thousands of people cooperate in the creation of the city, there must be some practical system of rules or procedures, which allows people to approach at least an approximation of the one rule, so that they can get on with the practical task of building.]

In our experiment, we ourselves after all experienced this difficulty, too. The graduate students who played the role of citizens, within our simulation, also knew very little of this one rule. Yet, within a matter of weeks, we (CA and IK) had to find a way of communicating something substantial to them, so that they could begin their work, make proposals for building projects, and carry out these projects, in our simulated urban development.

In order to solve this problem, we invented seven simpler rules . . . rules that we may call intermediate rules. These rules were concrete and clear. They gave people instructions about what to do, and how to do it. The instructions given, allowed people, to varying degrees, to approach the meaning of the one rule, and to make, in some fashion, more or less limited, some kind of wholeness.

These seven intermediate rules—actually each one is *itself* a system of several subrules—help to make the one rule concrete, and make it feasible to implement the one rule, from day to day. /

(Let us understand clearly how the seven rules embody the one rule.

We have already said that the overriding rule requires only one thing:'That every act of construction, every increment of growth in the city, works towards the creation of wholeness.)More fully, the one rule will require the following of the urban process:¸Every increment of construction in the growing city must be designed to preserve wholeness at all levels, from the largest level of public space, to the intermediate wholes at the scale of individual buildings, to the smallest wholes that occur in the building details.)

The seven rules, quite simply then, try to make sure that this happens. They are practical, and easily implementable rules, whose application will embody the one rule.

The seven rules were worked out empirically during a series of preliminary studies, not reported in this book. They were formulated, and tested, one by one, on various minor simulations. Once we were sure that each one by itself worked, more or less, then we incorporated it in the "big" experiment which is reported in Part two of this book.

So these intermediate rules, are practical, efficient, and easy to use.

They exist at a variety of levels, like the rules of organization in a growing organism.

29

But they are *intermediate* rules, because they are, at best, versions of the one rule. None of them is ultimately reliable. None of them can be repeated mechanically. None of them can be relied on to produce wholeness, without thought. At best, we can say that use of these intermediate rules gradually shows people how to make urban space whole.

But the more they understand these intermediate rules, the less necessary the rules are, and the more the users will approach a real understanding of the one rule.

The seven intermediate rules which we have defined are:

1. Piecemeal growth
2. The growth of larger wholes
3. Visions
4. The basic rule of positive urban space
5. Layout of large buildings
6. Construction
7. Formation of centers

As they stand, these seven rules are imperfectly formulated. Each one leaves much to be desired, both in its form, and in its detailed content. In any future attempt to carry out a real process of urban design, along the lines reported in this book, the seven intermediate rules will probably have to be improved considerably. They will also have to be adjusted according to local context.

However, we are fairly certain that the general range of these rules is correct, and that *some* version of these seven rules will always be needed, to embody the overriding rule correctly in a city.

CHAPTER 3

THE
SEVEN DETAILED
RULES OF GROWTH

RULE 1: PIECEMEAL GROWTH ~~&~~ Functional?

This rule establishes the piecemeal character of growth as a necessary precondition of wholeness. It does it by defining the small *size* of the increments. The rule is necessary simply because wholeness is too complicated to be built up in large lumps. The grain of development must be small enough, so that there is room, and time, for wholeness to develop.

It is necessary that the growth be piecemeal, and furthermore that *the idea of piecemeal growth be specified exactly enough so that we can guarantee a mixed flow of small, medium, and large projects in about equal quantities.*

In order to guarantee the piecemeal nature of the growth, this rule is made precise by three subrules:

1.1. The first subrule says that no building increment may be too large.

As an example, we specified that no single building increment could cost more than $5 million, or that no single building increment could have a floor area of more than 100,000 square feet. In practice, more subtle and more complex formulations would be needed.

1.2. The second subrule guarantees a reasonable mixture of sizes.

The detailed formulation of such a rule has been published in *The Oregon Experiment.* In the ideal version, the rule has a logarithmic character, which requires that the *total* amount of construction in small, medium, and large projects, is kept equal. In this ideal version, for every $3 million spent, $1 million will be spent on large projects (one project, say), $1 million will be spent on medium-sized projects (ten projects, say), and $1 million will be spent on small projects (a hundred projects, say).

However, the circumstances of our experiment would have made it impossible to follow this extreme rule, and we replaced it with a more modest one, namely: *There are equal numbers of large, medium, and small projects.*

This was practical for our experiment. However, of course, it still leaves a strong bias towards large projects, since the main volume of construction is still in large projects. Generally, some version of the rule between the two extremes would be best. For instance, 15 percent of all projects 10,000 to 100,000 square feet; 35 percent of all projects 1000 to 10,000 square feet; 50 percent of all projects less than 1000 square feet.

We may see the result of applying the version of the rule which we used in our experiment in the following graphic sequence. It shows the actual sequence of projects, by size.

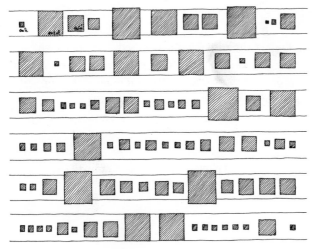

1.3. The third subrule guarantees a reasonable distribution of functions, in the piecemeal growth.

In a conventional master plan, different proportions of housing, manufacturing, public building and parking . . . are specified and guaranteed by the zoning ordinance. However, in a piecemeal process, it is conceivable that an entirely undesirable mix of functions might arise. This subrule is designed to create a reasonable balance among functions.

The rule simply requires that successive increments must be tailored to match an ideal distribution. Thus, for example:

Housing	26%
Shops and restaurants	7
Community functions	15
Hotels	5
Offices	16
Manufacturing	12
Parking	19

This is the distribution we used. Of course the ideal distribution would vary from community to community, according to the wishes of the community. In our project we wanted a very strong mix of functions.

In practice, this rule works as follows: an incremental count of running totals in each of these seven categories is kept. At each moment in time, *actual* running totals are either above or below the level specified by the ideal distribution. New projects which tend to move the actual distribution towards the ideal distribution, are encouraged. New projects which tend to move the actual distribution away from the ideal one are discouraged.

The following table shows the history of the project, at various stages, and shows how the flow of projects changed, as the actual distribution changed.

THE INCREMENTAL GROWTH IN 5 STAGES,
ACCORDING TO DIFFERENT FUNCTIONS

	Housing	Shops and Restaurants	Community Functions	Hotels	Offices	Manufacturing	Parking	Total Per Stage
1st stage project 1–14	55,225	79,646	98,705	98,300	117,550	38,600	100,000	588,026
2nd stage project 15–37	228,275	26,455	48,377	30,180	86,820	29,190	146,800	596,097
3rd stage project 38–56	103,456	32,054	137,922	0%	38,080	52,000	18,333	381,845
4th stage project 57–66	180,928	28,843	12,000	0%	108,824	63,778	220,000	614,373
5th stage project 67–89	119,246	20,622	114,838	12,000	73,629	130,584	9,024	479,943
Total Per Function	687,130	187,620	411,842	140,480	424,903	314,152	493,357	2,660,284
Total In %	25.82%	7.05%	15.48%	5.28%	15.97%	11.80%	18.54%	

The following diagram shows the same thing graphically:

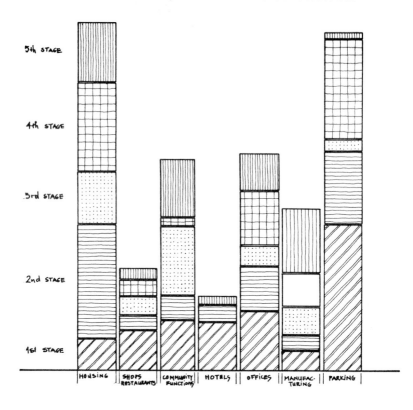

The distribution of sizes among the different projects in our simulation speaks for itself. However, to become completely aware of it, it is helpful to compare the size of the large hotel or theater (pp. 164, 182), the middle-sized houses and apartment buildings described in the grid (p. 172), and the many small fountains, benches, walls, and seats (pp. 136, 167, 226, 230).

Rule 2: The Growth of Larger Wholes

Piecemeal growth, by itself, will not create large wholes.

This is, of course, exactly why people produce plans. The intention of the "plan" is to create the larger wholes which are necessary to provide order and organization in the large.

The fact that the theory which is presented here tries to generate urban structure without a plan, is probably its most controversial feature.

However, in our experience, the kind of plan which is currently used, creates order at the expense of any organic feeling. Further, in a curious fashion, it is true to say that modern plans have completely failed to produce significant large scale order *anyway*.

This is partly because they are too inflexible to be implemented—a point discussed at length in *The Oregon Experiment*—but also partly because they are simply not capable of producing significant large-scale order, because they are not inspiring enough.

In the present theory, it is intended that *in some fashion*, the large-scale order will emerge, organically, from the co-operation of the individual acts of construction.

However, we must say right away that the precise extent of the control, or coordination which needs to be imposed on the individual acts, is not yet clear to us. This is the single greatest open question in the present theory. It is discussed further, on pages 243–249 of Part three.

For the purposes of our experiment, we chose a very flexible form of control over emerging larger wholes, which was roughly the following:

As the incremental acts of construction went forward, there was a continuing discussion about them, and about the larger wholes which seemed to be emerging under the surface.

At each stage, this discussion gradually yielded a common understanding of the large wholes that were indicated by the current thrust of development. This common understanding, which was shared by all the participants, was then injected into the next projects. The wholes which had been identified, began to grow.

However, at that stage, once again, there was evaluation and discussion of the larger wholes which seemed *actually* to be emerging—this was not always what had been predicted—and then, once again, the revised understanding was put back into the following increments.

There was thus a continuous process of feedback, between the individual projects and the informal process of defining larger wholes, until gradually, the small increments really did create the larger wholes.

However, there was almost never any explicit formulation of these large wholes as "targets." They were never drawn, for instance, only discussed. The large wholes which we tried to create, were the ones which appeared to be growing, organically, out of the process. They were never ones which were identified, artificially.

In practice, the rule governing this process was formulated as follows:

Every building increment must help to form at least one larger whole in the city, which is both larger and more significant than itself. Everyone managing a project must clearly identify which of the larger emerging wholes this project is trying to help, and how it will help to generate them.

To understand the way this process works, the following seven subrules are helpful:

2.1. In the process of growth, certain larger structures, or centers, emerge. These larger centers are distinct and recognizable entities, larger than any individual building. They are, essentially, the entities of public space that are formed by complexes or aggregates of buildings. Examples in our simulation are: the main square, the first mall, the small-grid streets, the great garden by the hotel, and the park-pier complex at the southern end.

2.2. These larger centers emerge slowly. That is, there is no one act of construction which totally produces one of these structures by itself. Each structure comes into being gradually.

2.3. These larger centers arise spontaneously. They are not planned ahead of time, but take shape gradually, and are always surprising, even to the people who have helped to create them.

2.4. However, *awareness* of these emerging centers, plays an essential role in the process by which they emerge. Each individual person who undertakes an act of construction, is always aware of the context of larger centers existing, emerging, and faintly hinted at on the horizon, and then shapes his own individual act, in such a way as to continue, and develop, this complex of emerging structures in the most satisfactory way.

2.5. Each of these larger centers has a very definite natural history, which goes through three phases. These phases are linked to the way that the individual acts of construction gradually create the wholes.

Phase 1. Some increment creates a hint of a new large center.

Phase 2. One or more additional increments then pinpoint the main outlines of its structure.

Phase 3. A series of further increments then complete the center.

Let us try to understand this by a few examples from our simulation.

Consider, for example, the pedestrian mall, at the beginning of the project.

1. This mall was first hinted at by the creation of the gateway (increment #1).

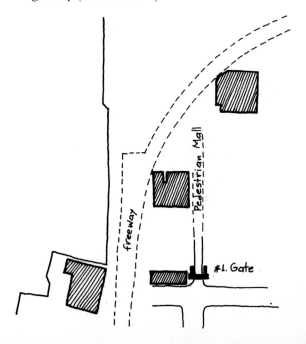

2. It was then defined and pinpointed by the hotel and the café (increments #2, #3) which fixed its right-hand side and hence its width, and by the community bank (increment #5), which fixed the position of the far end.

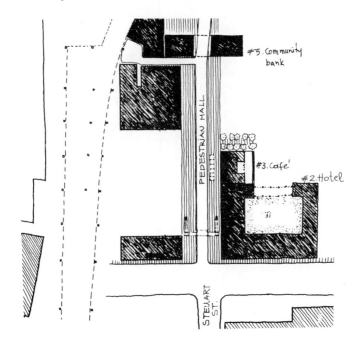

3. It was then completed by a series of increments including the apartment house (#7) and the office building (#9), which completed the definition of its boundary, and by various details such as the gravel walk and low wall (#21).

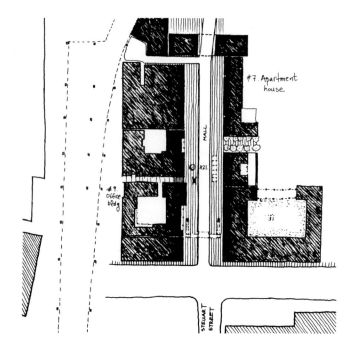

2.6. We may begin to see the complexity of the process when we recognize that any one increment of construction will usually play simultaneous, but different roles, with respect to *different* larger centers.

For example, the gateway, which was the very first increment in our experiment, already played these three roles as follows:

First, it helped to *define* the activity node or space at the intersection of the bus station, Mission Street and Steuart Street.

42

Second, it helped to *complete* the development of Mission Street, as a whole.

Third, it created the *hint* of a new pedestrian mall, going south from it.

The second increment, the hotel, did the same:

First, it began to *pin down* the pedestrian mall, by fixing its west boundary line.

Second, it helped to *complete* both Mission Street, and the same node that the gateway pins down, simply by forming the corner.

Third, it created the *hint* of a new structure, which was later to become the public garden. The hint was not automatic. In fact, we had to modify the hotel to create a hint in the following way: when first proposed, the garden was entirely closed to the south. We refused to allow this, on the grounds that it was too shut in, and did not reach out or help to embrace the larger site. After our modification, the garden was left with a slight opening to the south, under a trellis. And we saw, then, the possibility of a larger garden, a very large public garden, to the south, which opened from the smaller hotel garden.

In general, each new increment x does all three things:

1. X always helps to complete at least one major center which is already clearly defined.
2. X usually plays a role in pinning down some other, less clearly defined center, which has so far only been hinted at by earlier increments of construction.

43

3. X usually creates a hint, of some entirely new larger center, which will emerge fully, only in much later increments.

In this sense, each valid increment of construction plays a role in at least three larger centers, to which it contributes, and gives form.

We see, then, that the web of interactions between increments, and the larger centers which they help to form, is enormously complex.

2.7. In addition, the total number of the larger centers is surprisingly great. For instance, although there are only about a dozen really important major centers in our experiment, there are, all in all, perhaps seventy larger centers which play a role in making the communal space coherent . . . almost as many as there are individual building increments.

The wholeness of the environment is formed by this very large number of larger centers, all interwoven, interlaced, and overlapping, in the most intricate way.

The following sequence of maps from our experiment shows the incremental growth of larger urban structures— the mall, the garden, the main square, the grid. The way these large wholes emerged is described in the second part of the book.

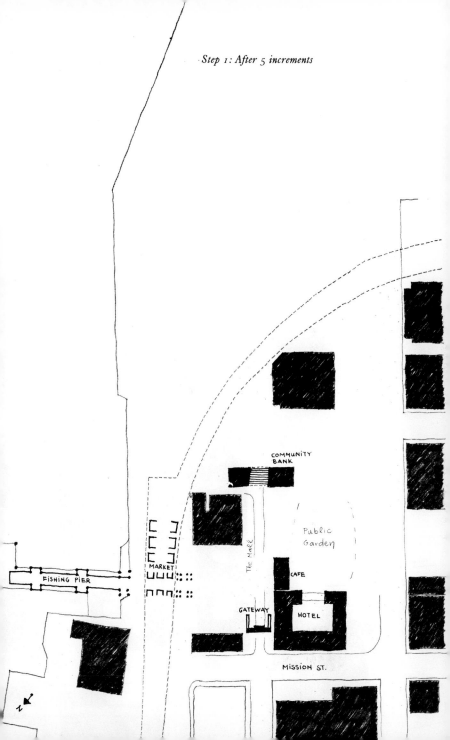

Step 1: After 5 increments

FISHING PIER

MARKET

COMMUNITY BANK

Public Garden

The Mall

CAFE

GATEWAY

HOTEL

MISSION ST.

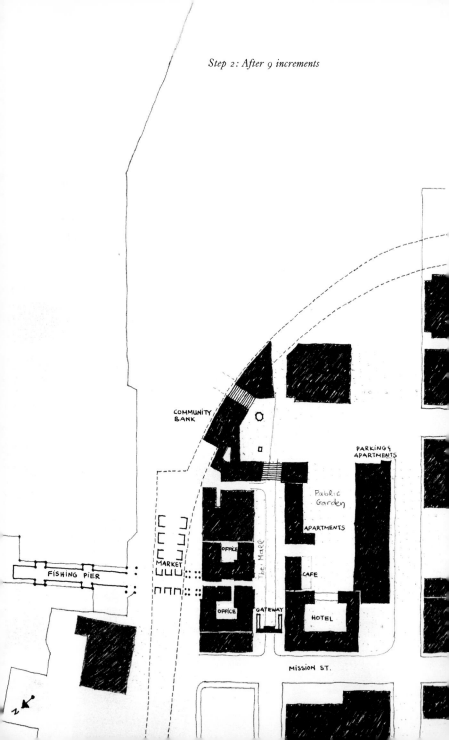

Step 2: After 9 increments

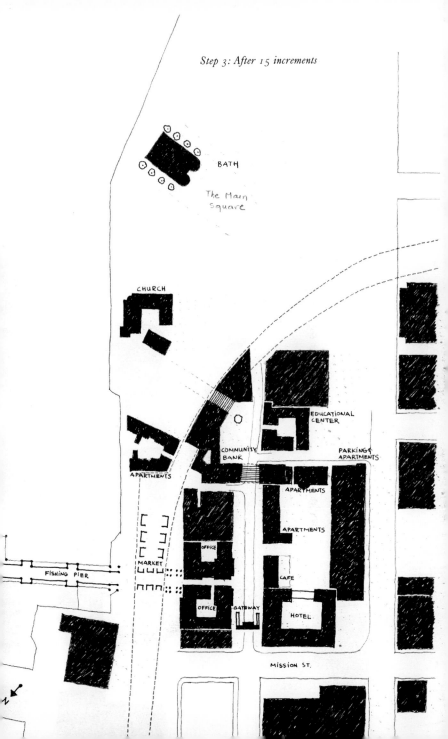

Step 3: After 15 increments

BATH

The Main
Square

CHURCH

EDUCATIONAL
CENTER

COMMUNITY
BANK

PARKING &
APARTMENTS

APARTMENTS

APARTMENTS

APARTMENTS

OFFICE

FISHING PIER

MARKET

CAFE

OFFICE

GATEWAY

HOTEL

MISSION ST.

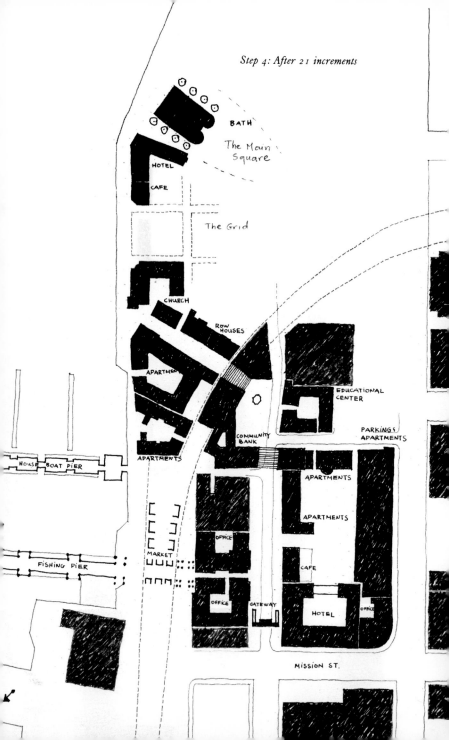

Step 4: After 21 increments

BATH

The Main
Square

HOTEL

CAFE

The Grid

CHURCH

ROW
HOUSES

APARTMENTS

EDUCATIONAL
CENTER

PARKING &
APARTMENTS

HOUSE BOAT PIER

APARTMENTS

COMMUNITY
BANK

APARTMENTS

APARTMENTS

OFFICE

MARKET

FISHING PIER

CAFE

OFFICE

GATEWAY

HOTEL

OFFICE

MISSION ST.

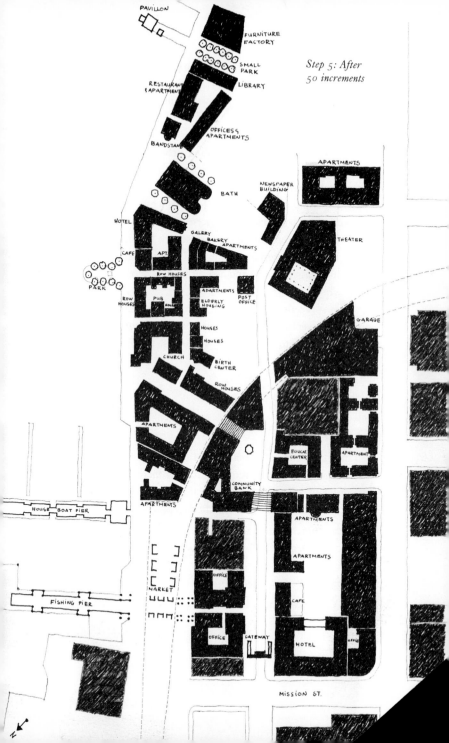

PAVILLON

FURNITURE FACTORY

SMALL PARK

RESTAURANT & APARTMENT

LIBRARY

Step 5: After 50 increments

OFFICES & APARTMENTS

BANDSTAND

APARTMENTS

NEWSPAPER BUILDING

BATH

THEATER

HOTEL

GALERY
BAKERY
APARTMENTS

CAFE

APT.

ROW HOUSES

PARK

ROW HOUSES

PUB

HOUSE

APARTMENTS

POST OFFICE

ELDERLY HOUSING

GARAGE

HOUSES

HOUSES

CHURCH

BIRTH CENTER

ROW HOUSES

APARTMENTS

EDUCAT CENTER

APARTMENT

COMMUNITY BANK

HOUSE BOAT PIER

APARTMENTS

APARTMENTS

APARTMENTS

MARKET

OFFICE

FISHING PIER

CAFE

OFFICE

GATEWAY

HOTEL

OFFICE

MISSION ST.

N

We must make it clear that we are not sure that the method of forming larger wholes which we have proposed here is powerful enough.

In our experience of simulating urban growth, and trying to produce wholeness in the experiment, we found that the most consistent error, the most consistent blindness—whether of the people concerned, or of the process—*was always the blindness to large structure.* Piecemeal growth tends, in spite of all good intentions and promises, to be piecemeal in the *bad* sense, incoherent, scattered, fragmented. It tends to produce aggregations and assemblies . . . instead of coherent wholes.

To solve this problem, it may be necessary to use still more powerful methods of generating large wholes, and linking them to the piecemeal process. This is discussed in Part three.

RULE 3: VISIONS

This rule defines the *content* and *character* of the individual increments. The rule requires that the increments arise from a *vision* of what is needed to heal the existing structure, not from an intellectually formed concept. Thus:

Every project must first be experienced, and then expressed, as a vision which can be seen in the inner eye (literally). It must have this quality so strongly that it can also be communicated to others, and felt by others, as a vision.

We have found, in various earlier experiments which

50

preceded the main experiment reported in this book, that the substance of any growth in the city, can be either "authentic" or not . . . heartfelt or not . . . coming from human impulses . . . or not. ⧫

In our experience, wholeness can never be created unless the individual acts of construction are governed by such human impulses and human content.

We are not referring here to some kind of socialistic concern with humanitarian programs and community welfare. This kind of thing, though valuable—and crucial when it is missing—can by itself produce misery and *lack* of wholeness, just as much as capitalistic concern with money can produce these things.

What we are talking about is a much deeper level of human meaning. We have found that the increments of development will not produce wholeness, unless they come from a sort of dreamlike quality . . . unless they come from a childlike, almost childish quality of directness, direct concern for life . . . unless, in short, they are genuinely based on human visions. ⧫

Formulated as a rule, every project, then, must first be experienced, and then expressed *as a vision, which can be seen (literally, in the inner eye), communicated to others, and felt by others . . . as a vision.* ⧫

In practical terms, this vision must come into play *before anything else* . . . that is to say, at that moment when the project is first formulated, first conceived.

The vision is an answer to the fundamental question: *What* shall we build in any given place, where a project is to be undertaken. This question does not ask how it is or-

51

ganized, how it is designed, what character the architecture has . . . but simply the most fundamental question of all: *What is it? What is going to be there?*

In today's development, this question is asked, and answered, almost exclusively in economic terms. What can pay for itself there? What can make money there?

Of course the products which are built, in answer to this question, and after the necessary consumer surveys, are machinelike, abstract, lifeless. They are uninteresting, not vivid. They are incapable of exciting us, or moving us, because they are not human in their quality.

If we compare these modern corporate and socialistic products with the buildings made in other ages, we see that buildings made in other times have an entirely different character.

Even in the immediate past—the period of great industrialization, of filth, and money, and slave labor—there is still a quality which is more inspiring than what we have today. Consider, for example, the stockyards of Chicago, the Loop, the New York waterfront, the coal mines of the Rhonda Valley in Wales, Les Halles in Paris. There is, in all these cases, a thrust, an excitement, a vision. . . .

In each of these cases, we might question the vision, we might have doubts about its social value. But it was, nonetheless, undeniably human. It was the product of a personal vision. Even when it concerned money and profit, it was still in some terms a vision of betterment, a vision of value, seen by an individual, and carried out with force.

By comparison, the developments of today, are not human in their origin. They are too often created by corpora-

tions who manipulate stock for profit at long distance, or decided by committees concerned with abstract social welfare. They are too often grey and colorless.

If we turn to earlier times, we find visions of much greater force, and greater purity. For instance, the great bridge of Isphahan, where Shah Abbas decided to build a place of enjoyment, where the people of the city could live and play on the water, is a product of a vision. The story of his appointing the architect, under pain of death, and visiting him disguised as a beggar, to make sure that his work was being correctly carried out, is typical of its visionary character.

In earlier times, even the simplest acts, done on an ordinary farm, had the qualities of visions.

Compare, for example, a farmer coming down to breakfast one day, and saying to his family: "Well, I think it's time we built a bridge over the big creek, before the winter rains come . . . ," with the decision of the Berkeley Public Works department to build a culvert over a stream which is flooding a certain street.

The farmer's act is an act of vision. He presents it in this way to his family. They carry it like that in their minds. And they build it like that.

The bridge which the Public Works Department builds is something entirely different. It is arrived at not as a result of vision, but as a result of considered, channelled, information. Studies are prepared. Each member of the engineer's team carefully protects himself against possible criticism, and minces words in his report. It is built, in the end, purely as a bureaucratic act, entirely *without* vision.

This vision is a literal thing. It is not merely an idea or concept, but a thing seen and felt in the mind's eye as in a dream, perhaps literally seen in a dream. *And as a result it has intensely personal feeling.* It makes some feeling manifest, it carries us on a wave of life, makes us feel life, black, grey, or brilliant . . . but still it is life, in the Chicago stockyards, or in the shrine of Ise in Japan. They are all, above all, personal visions, carrying something from far beyond . . . never merely the product of bureaucratic messages.

∽ ✛ ∽

We must emphasize that visions are *necessary* for producing wholeness.

The importance of a vision does not merely lie in the humanity, the human reality of what is seen in the inner eye. The vision is mainly vital, in the end, because it is *more accurate.* It produces what is needed to produce wholeness in a given situation, more accurately, than any intellectual process.

Within the piecemeal process, if each act of construction is going to contribute to wholeness, then the main thing, above all others, is that this act must grow, naturally and directly, *from what is there already.*

This may seem obvious. However, in "normal" present-day urban growth it is not the rule at all. Today, most typically, each person or corporation owns a piece of land. They consider, often for years, what they should do with this piece of land . . . and, of course, in present-day society, their thought is most often governed by the question of what action will make most money there.

Clearly, this motive is not the same as the one which seeks wholeness.

Even if we leave money and profit aside, it is still clear that the decision usually taken is one which looks inward, only to the good of the individual piece of land, and does not at all look outward, to seek the good of the surrounding city.

This is not because motives are selfish. It is because the modes of thought we usually employ do not help to identify those actions which will do most to heal the larger whole. The reason is this: most actions are governed by concepts, by *ideas* of what may be good. These concepts, ideas, and

58

solutions arrived at by calculation are, most often, not deeply related to the existing structure . . . simply because the modes of thought are not subtle enough to create a relation of this kind.

In order to see the whole, it is necessary to enter into a more fundamental, and more primitive relation to the question. And the mode of thought which is most capable of creating and identifying relationships to the whole, is precisely the one which we call "visionary."

∽ ✛ ∽

We shall understand all this most clearly by finally discussing the *timing* of a vision, and the way that the "next" project always depends, for its details, on the moment in time sequence when it is first imagined.

The following passage is one of many which we gave to our students to clarify the rules while the experiment was going on:

March 26, 1979

In looking over the various proposals which you have made so far, I realize that there is one crucial aspect of the process which I have not yet made clear—and which, as far as I can see, almost none of you have so far understood.

So far, almost all your proposals, even when they are based on a genuine inner vision in your mind, are still essentially solitary. What I mean by that, is that they exist more or less independently of their surroundings.

You will see this, if you realize that almost all your visions or proposals have so far been independent of the

60

exact moment in the sequence when they occur.

For example, suppose your proposal is the nth increment in the whole sequence. Then there has been a sequence of previous increments P_1, P_2, P_3 . . . leading up to P_n, your proposal.

Although your proposal has usually had general relevance to some of what has come before (to P_1, P_2, and P_3), it still tends to float as a proposal, independent of whether it is precisely P_n or P_{n+1}. In other words, as far as you are concerned, your proposal is valid according to its general relationships to the overall site. But not one of you has realized yet, that your proposal should be enormously sensitive to the *exact* moment in sequence when it comes, and that a certain proposal might make sense as P_n, if it comes after P_{n-1}, but as soon as even one other proposal comes in between, even in a place fairly far away from that location, then a properly executed project at the place where P_n was will have to be enormously different from P_n.

It is even possible that the whole idea of what you proposed as P_n might no longer be relevant at all—because as a result of P_{n-1}, the gestalt of the whole has shifted so enormously.

Let me explain all this another way. At any given moment in the evolution of the site, there is a certain configuration there. It consists of everything that has been built, up to that moment. If we are now going to try to make a "next" proposal, we must ask ourselves, "What proposal, and where placed, and how formed, will now do the most to make the whole area more complete, more whole, AS A TOTALITY."

We are able to ask such a question, because we can pay attention to the site in its present state, "listen" with our inner ear for the gaps, for the lack of wholeness, for its most essential incompleteness, and then do what we can to mend it, by doing one thing which does more than any other to make *the entire project* more whole.

This is the essence of any authentic vision. The failure to understand this will always make visions strange, or egocentric, or weird. An authentic vision comes into your mind, because it springs from the understanding of the whole, it presents itself to you, as the completion of the whole, as the form of life, the place, the organization which does most to bring the entire thing to life, still more, as a totality.

And the implication of this attitude is, of course, that you ask yourself what to do next, at each point, as though there is *one* best answer, and you are listening, trying to find that answer. This does not mean that there always is one best answer. There may be two or three perhaps, almost equally good. But your mental attitude, at each moment, must be, "What is *the* single best thing that I can do now, at this moment, to bring the whole to life."

This means, of course, that what you propose at time P_n, for a given area of the project, will be different from what you would propose a moment later, after one more project has been added, because the gestalt of the whole has changed and what is needed now, to make the whole complete, is entirely different from what it was the moment before.

When you understand this properly, then finally you will

realize that in this process, there is little room for anything which is personal in the egocentric sense . . . because you merely become the vehicle, the medium, through which the demands of the site speak, and make themselves felt . . . and your vision is a product of the inner shouting of the site, not a product of your whimsy or your fantasy. . . .

But to the extent that your inner ear is accurate, to the extent that you can listen to what the project in its totality is calling for, you will produce something far more wonderful than anything you could dream of by trying to be original.

ოు **✤** ოు

For an example of a building which clearly comes from a vision, it is useful to study the bath, on page 142. For a minor example of a less imposing building, but one also very strongly based on a vision, the small post office on page 189 is very helpful.

Rule 4: Positive Urban Space

Once a vision has defined the life and activity which is to occur in some new increment of growth, this vision must be embodied in a physical design.

To make this design whole, it is absolutely essential that the space created by the buildings have a positive character.

This is difficult to grasp, because, in our time, urban space has become negative . . . the leftover . . . after buildings are built. However, in all cultures which pro-

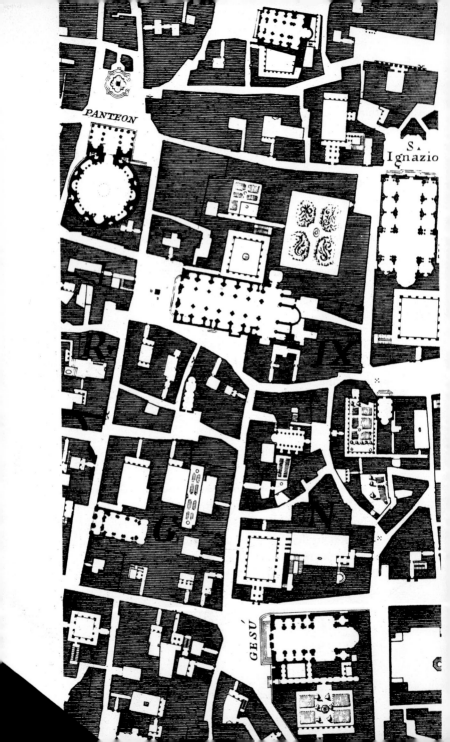

PANTEON

S.
Ignazio

GESÚ

duced great cities and buildings, space was understood as a positive thing created *by* the buildings.

The rule says simply:

Every building must create coherent and well-shaped public space next to it.

To make this idea easy to understand, we have formulated a set of rules which identify five types of elements—pedestrian space, buildings, gardens, streets, and parking—and then prescribe the necessary relationships between these elements.

In essence, the rules guarantee that the pedestrian space, gardens, streets, and parking spaces, are formed *by* the buildings, not vice-versa. The space becomes the main focus of attention, and the buildings become merely the tools with which this all-important space is created. This reverses the situation which we have today, where buildings, not space, are the main focus of attention.

Thus the buildings explicitly become the creators of the urban space.

The five subrules are:

4.1. Each time a building increment is built, it is shaped and placed in such a way that it creates well-shaped pedestrian space.

4.2. The building volume of the increment is itself also simple and well-shaped.

4.3. Often (but not always) the building will also be shaped to create a garden. This garden will also be a compact and simple shape, but more intimate and quiet than the nearby pedestrian space.

66

4.4. The nearest road is also extended to give direct access to the building . . . unless the building is already touching an existing road.

4.5. A tally is kept of total available parking space. If there are not enough nearby parking spaces, a new parking garage must also be built, within 500 feet, and the building is always placed in such a way as to shield the parking.

We now explain each of these five subrules in detail, to make them absolutely clear.

4.1. *Each time a building increment is built, it is shaped and placed in such a way that it creates well-shaped pedestrian space.*

We may express this rule simply as follows: "Buildings surround space," NOT "Space surrounds buildings." It has become a habit of thought in our century that buildings are simple-shaped volumes, floating in a sea of ill-formed space. If we compare a plan of a typical modern city, with, for

instance, the great Nolli plan of Rome, as shown on page 64, we see there that it is the *space* which is made up of simply-formed shapes, while the buildings are more irregular, loose relaxed shapes, whose primary function is to surround and shape their space.

a. First of all, this means that each building is placed in a position where, together with other existing buildings, it forms exterior space which is beautifully dimensioned and shaped. This choice of position dominates the building and its design.

Piazza San Marco

b. It may also begin to define new pedestrian space, which will be finished later . . . by the cooperation of other building increments, not yet built.

68

c. In particular, a building must tend to create a system of nodes and streets. The nodes are small, open squares, perhaps 60 to 100 feet in diameter. These nodes are, on the average, about 300 feet apart, and are connected by pedestrian streets and lanes.

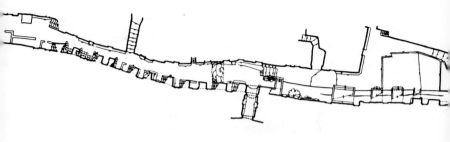

The shape of a path

d. According to the importance of the building, and its location, each building creates space of a different size, so that there is a clear gradient of sizes in the pedestrian spaces which are created.

4.2. *The building volume itself is also simply and beautifully shaped.*

a. This means that the building volume is itself a simple and compact unity, or is made up of several simple compact volumes—one of these being major, and the others minor, hanging onto it.

69

b. The main entrance of the building forms a natural
   center, and is highly visible from nearby pedestrian areas.

c. The volume is pierced by "holes" that are either
   gardens, or courtyards, or lightwells—and no wing
   of the building is more than about 40 feet thick.

d. If possible, the building touches at least one other existing building, so that the buildings together form a continuous fabric throughout the city.

e. The building has at least one wall which has no windows, so that other buildings may later also be built touching *it*.

71

    f. If possible, the building is built in a position which helps to shield some parking area, or parking garage, so that it does double duty as a shield.

4.3. *At intervals, between the buildings, there are gardens. These are also carefully shaped and follow the general rule 4.1 for positive space.*

Such gardens are only added, when they make sense, functionally, with the building, and when they are added, they represent the quiet, more private side of open space.

Such a garden follows these principles:

    a. It is always on the south of the buildings which it most obviously serves.

b. It is never next to roads, or parking lots.

c. Each garden itself has a beautiful shape, and is attractive . . . not merely as a "piece" of green but as an ornament . . . with its own lawns, flowers, trees, forming a clear and beautiful structure in itself.

4.4. *As each new building is built, the roads nearby are extended, incrementally, to give vehicular access to that building.*

73

Roads serve buildings

Roads are built, incrementally, as they are needed, to serve buildings. If there is already a road touching the proposed building site, no new increment needs to be built. If there is no road serving the building, then a new section of road needs to be built, with certain principles in mind:

The principle that roads are built incrementally, to serve buildings, and fitted to the buildings after the buildings are conceived, not before, is of *immense* importance.

We insisted on this rule during the experiment, simply because present-day urban development is ruined, most often, by the hierarchy of decisions in which the road network comes first, buildings come second, and pedestrian space comes third.

74

The correct sequence, as we are trying to show in this system of rules, is just the opposite: pedestrian space first, buildings second, and roads *third*.

We realize that this subrule is perhaps the single most questionable rule in the experiment as formulated here. And we found, as may be expected, that this form of the rule does not necessarily generate a coherent network of roads.

It was nevertheless amazing to what extent an orderly network of roads *did* result within the experiment, so we therefore leave the rule unedited.

Further comments on this topic are made in Part three.

4.5. *Parking space is the last element in the hierarchy, and must also be placed so that buildings surround it, and its effect on the environment is reduced as far as possible.*

At each increment a check is made of parking requirements. If additional parking space is needed, a garage or parking lot must be built, in an appropriate position, to meet the newly generated parking needs, according to the following principles:

a. The parking lot, or garage, is always "buried" or half buried within a building, so that the buildings surround the parking spaces, or are built up against them, to shield them as far as possible.

b. In general, a parking garage is made up of strips which are 60 feet wide, and the total width of the structure may be any multiple, thus 60, 120, 180. . . .

c. Each car requires a total of 300 square feet of space, so there are two cars for every 10 feet of such a 60-foot-wide strip.

75

d. Often it is economical to build a large garage, perhaps filling an awkward corner. Because of this, a garage built, will often be far larger than the particular building increment warrants. At the time of construction, each garage thus has a surplus of unused spaces. As later increments are built, this surplus is reduced, increment by increment, until there is again no available parking, and a new garage has to be built.

d. The parking garage serving any particular building increment must always be within 500 feet of that building.

e. Parking must always, of course, connect with a road.

f. When you leave a parking structure, you can always see the entrances of the building which the parking structure serves.

ᴏⱳ ✛ ᴏⱳ

Examples of the rules of urban space, and their application, will be found throughout the simulation. However, the formation of the theater, as a way of completing the main square (p. 184), is a very good example of the way a building uses pedestrian space.

The formation of a garden, as an adjunct to a building, will be found on page 152.

The construction of a parking structure, under the conditions of Rule 4.5 is most clearly described on page 156.

76

And the gradual formation of a vehicular road, winding through the middle of the project, in response to various building increments, can be seen on pages 114, 128, and 183.

RULE 5: LAYOUT OF LARGE BUILDINGS

Now we come to the design and layout of the buildings themselves. We cannot expect to have wholeness in the large, wholeness in the city or the neighborhood, if the buildings themselves are unwhole internally. Thus, although the internal layout of buildings would normally not be considered as part of the domain of planning or urban design, we cannot avoid having to influence, and modify, the layout of the buildings which make up the city—at least enough so that they are sufficiently whole, within themselves, to produce wholeness next to them. Specifically:

The entrances, the main circulation, the main division of the building into parts, its interior open spaces, its daylight, and the movement within the building, are all coherent and consistent with the position of the building in the street and in the neighborhood.

We have formulated a precise process for laying out the buildings, in such a way that these elements become well ordered, and well integrated. The project in our experiment which embodies this sequence, most clearly, is the education center, page 137. We use it here as an example. The steps are to be used in sequence:

5.1. As part of the public space process, determine the site of the building, its frontage, and its approximate ground plan.

5.2. With knowledge of the total square footage needed in the building, and the height of neighboring buildings, decide the number of storeys.

5.3. If the building has a main part, identify the location and height (and therefore the volume) of the main mass of the building.

5.4. Determine the position of the main courtyard (if there is one) and any other courtyards.

5.5. Determine the position of any major gardens, and make sure that their position is such that they will get a reasonable amount of sunlight.

5.6. Identify the subsidiary parts of the building as subsidiary masses.

5.7. Determine the main direction of approach to the building from nearby pedestrian streets, and fix the position of the main entrance.

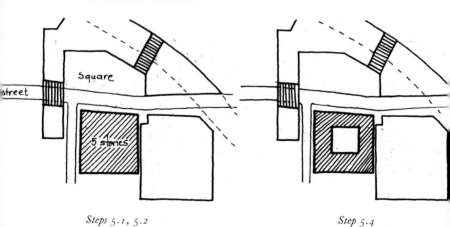

Steps 5.1, 5.2   *Step 5.4*

5.8. Locate the entrance lobby as a major space inside the entrance. This lobby may be very large, and more than one storey high.

5.9. Locate indoor streets, if there are any, as major streets at least two storeys high inside the building. In general, these indoor streets must be top-lit, and therefore glazed.

5.10. If there are now any volumes of the building left, which are more than 40 feet wide, introduce light wells in appropriate places, so that the building is made up of wings, lit from both sides, and never more than 40 feet wide.

5.11. Locate all other major interior spaces, which have the same order of magnitude as the lobby . . . this would include, for instance, auditoria, main meeting rooms, ballrooms, gymnasia, major waiting rooms, etc. In general, after this stage, all major public spaces have been located.

5.12. Place the main staircase (and elevator if there is one) in the building. Remember that this stair is essentially a volume of space several storeys high, not merely a diagonal line . . . so treat the staircase as an open room with a stair around the edge of it.

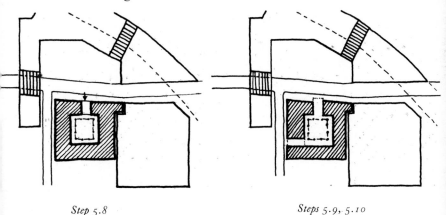

Step 5.8   *Steps 5.9, 5.10*

5.13. Place windowed galleries or open arcades around those courtyards which are to serve as major circulation spaces, or leave circulation on the ground, but always arrange access to these courtyards so that the main lobby leads to all of them in a clear manner.

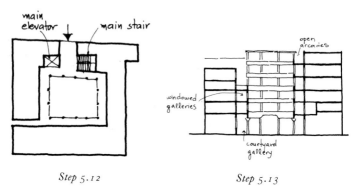

Step 5.12   *Step 5.13*

5.14. If parts of the ground floor are to be used for shops or public functions, with direct access to the street, identify the parts which are to be used this way.

5.15. Within the building, identify certain "nodes of intensity" at key points in the circulation system. This means, certain natural gathering spots (coffee shops, tobacco shops, gift shops, food stores, bars, garden seats) should be placed at spots where all paths in the building come together, so that they naturally invite gathering, and activity.

5.16. Determine the relative size of all the different departments (or apartments . . . whatever natural subunits are expected in the building), and distribute them in the different parts of the building. If these departments belong

80

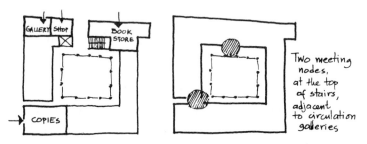

Step 5.14   Step 5.15

to identifiable groups of users, then allow them to choose locations in the building. Units do not have to be confined to one floor. Often it will be very good to have units occupying vertical swaths or three-dimensional chunks of space in the building.

5.17. If any department or apartment has its own roof terrace, and therefore opens out onto the roof of a lower part of the building, define these terraces clearly now, so that variations in the heights of the building are fully understood at this stage.

5.18. Wherever vertical seams exist between departments, make it clear how these seams will become visible in the finished building. It is probably useful to imagine that a well-defined, and at least partially visible structural entity, should coincide with each department . . . and you should begin to know how the traces of these various structural entities will be visible on the outside of the building. Apartments, for example, should be visible as entities from the outside, and from the direction of approach. If the departments are vertical departments, the buildings should be visible as slender high buildings (the Amsterdam solution).

81

5.19. Now locate the secondary stairs and elevators which serve the departments. These stairs must connect with the main lobby, via the system of galleries which has already been created. For the apartments, the stairs may be exterior to the building. For some offices, the stairs may give access to the ground in such a way that they are directly accessible from the outside . . . but the stairs must always be easily explained to a person who goes first to the main entrance of the building, without having to backtrack.

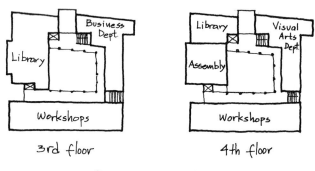

Steps 5.16, 5.17, 5.18, 5.19

5.20. Locate the entrance of each department so that it can be seen from the stairs, and make this entrance a major volume, easily identifiable, and leading to a clear sense of orientation within the department, as one enters it. This entrance should always lead one to a position looking out over an outdoor area, so that one moves naturally towards the light.

5.21. Within each department, define the largest and most important room, or rooms, and place these rooms with great care, so that they have beautiful light, and are in a suitable position with respect to access, views out, sunlight, and the natural hierarchy of space in the department. In many cases these "large" rooms may have higher ceilings than other rooms.

5.22. Define the major chains of rooms, next in importance to the large rooms. Again, place these chains with special care for the light. Do not worry too much about space for circulation. Instead allow these rooms to provide circulation leading from one room to the next. If these rooms are to have lower ceilings than the largest rooms, then begin to consider possible ways in which the structure of the department (seen as a load-bearing system) can produce the necessary variations in height.

5.23. If the department has more than one floor, now place its internal stairs.

5.24. Place any small passages necessary to give access to rooms within the department.

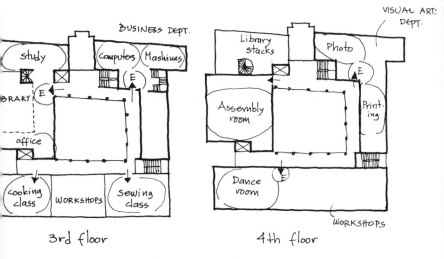

Steps 5.20, 5.21, 5.22, 5.23

5.25. Finally place small rooms, individual rooms, bathrooms, storerooms etc, in the small spaces left by previous decisions.

RULE 6: CONSTRUCTION

This rule deals with the *details* of the buildings. Even if a building is laid out well, in such a fashion that its volume is well formed, and in such a fashion that its internal layout is well formed, its wholeness, and the wholeness of the space around it, will still depend to a great degree on the wholeness of the building details, and on the wholeness of the structure of the building.

The physical construction of the buildings themselves, cannot be separated from the wholeness of the city. Jerusalem has a well-known ordinance which requires that every building must be faced with stone. A bit extreme perhaps, and grossly formulated. But the basic point is perfectly clear. The wholeness of a city cannot be separated from the wholeness of the construction used to make its buildings.

The structure of every building must generate smaller wholes in the physical fabric of the building, in its structural bays, columns, walls, windows, building base, etc.—in short, in its entire physical construction and appearance.

This rule contains a series of very roughly formulated rules of thumb, which can help to guarantee the well-formed character and wholeness of the building structure and details.

The rules stand at two levels:

A. The first set of rules is concerned with the global three-dimensional organization of the building structure. These rules guarantee that the physical structure will be in harmony with the volumes and spaces of the building.

B. The second set of rules is concerned with details. These rules guarantee that the exterior of the building will be in harmony with the exterior public space.

A. *Global structure*

In order to produce a coherent structure in the building, we require that each building have a clear global organization of structure at three levels of scale: structural bays, primary structure, and secondary structure.

6.1. Configuration of structural bays

The fundamental unit of the structural scheme is a unit which we may loosely call a "structural bay." A structural bay is a three-dimensional structural element, which exists, or could exist, as a structural entity by itself, in three dimensions. A structural bay may be several storeys high, but it is bounded by major columns, beams, and walls.

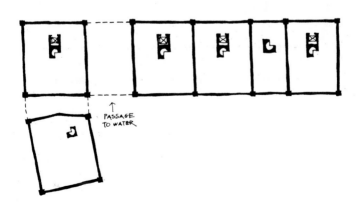

PASSAGE
TO WATER

At an early stage, during the first layout of a building, it is necessary to begin visualizing the building as a configuration of structural bays. We might say that the configuration of structural bays is the first structural sketch of the building.

We require that the configuration of structural bays be visible both inside and outside the building.

6.2. Primary structure

Within the structural bays, there are primary columns and beams. However, the primary columns and beams are not necessarily consistent from one bay to the next. This means that there can be variation of column spacing, and ceiling height, within different structural bays.

The primary structure defines the largest rooms and spaces within the building.

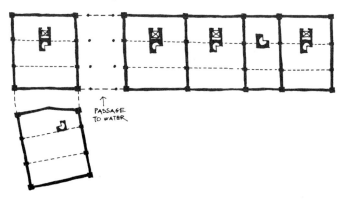

PASSAGE
TO WATER

We require that the largest rooms and spaces be bounded by primary columns and beams, so that the primary structure is consistent with the largest spaces, and so that they can be read, inside and outside, directly from the elements which form the primary structure.

6.3. Secondary structure

Minor rooms and passages, are defined by secondary structural elements. These may include walls, smaller columns and beams, and ceilings.

The secondary beams and columns, typically span between primary beams and columns.

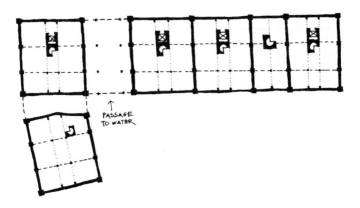

PASSAGE
TO WATER

The following schematic example shows a two-storey superbay with different floor plans. The primary and secondary structures of the two floors work harmoniously together. All primary columns of the second floor are aligned with the beam structure of the first floor.

87

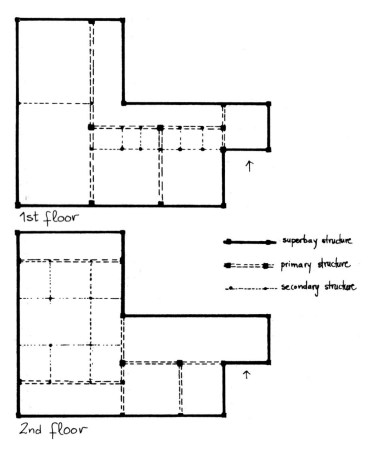

1st floor

2nd floor

superbay structure
primary structure
secondary structure

The structure of a superbay

B. Details

Within the broad scheme of the structure defined by these three rules, we require that each building follow some version of the following rules for details:

6.4. Base storey. There is a base storey, which is higher than others, and is marked by a larger, grander, structure.

6.5. Roof line. There is a roof line, marked by ornament, parapet, or something else distinct; the whole thing at least four feet high.

6.6. Differentiation. The floors are differentiated by level, with a gradient of window size, floor height, or spacing of structural elements, according to the following scheme: 1—different, 2 and 3—maybe the same, 3 and 4, or 4 by itself—different again, and top—different.

6.7. All buildings have distinct windows, with visible window frames.

6.8. The total area of window, measured to outside of frames, is between 30 and 50 percent of the total wall area.

6.9. There is some additional structure, either ornament or substructure, visible at the same scale as the window frames—or it might be smaller.

6.10. All buildings are made of reinforced concrete or masonry (laid-up concrete blocks), painted or plastered, or left natural. There are no prefabricated concrete elements larger than blocks or beams.

6.11. Bay sizes within one building are the same, except where there are specific and powerful reasons for changing them.

For an example of a building which follows these rules exactly, both for global structure and for details, it is useful to study the warehouse on page 216.

View from the water

North elevation of main square

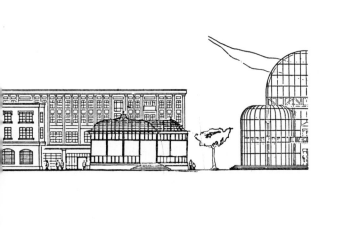

RULE 7: FORMATION OF CENTERS

This rule deals with the geometric shape of *all* the wholes, at all scales within the process. It is the closest thing we have to an explicit formulation of the one rule, but as concrete and usable as possible.

It describes certain geometric rules of thumb which will make sure that a building as a volume, or any increment of a building, or even any small detail, is capable of cooperating with the space adjacent to it, and capable of making wholes which include both the building and the space.

This rule makes use, directly, of results which are internal to the nature of the one rule (taken from the manuscript "The Nature of Order"). It introduces specific geometric rules, in a highly simplified form, which are rather easy to follow, even though not entirely accurate.

Every whole must be a "center" in itself, and must also produce a system of centers around it.

This principle hinges on the definition of a "center." In order to understand this concept in detail, we may set down the following specific principles:

Definition of a center

7.1. A "thing," not a point. A center is not merely, as the word suggests, a point that happens to be a center of some larger field. A center is an entity; if you like, a "thing." It may be a building, an outdoor space, a garden, a wall, a road, a window, a complex of several of these at the same time.

7.2. Symmetry. In general, a center has some kind of ele-

mentary symmetry, especially bilateral symmetry, similar to that which the human body has; i.e., left-right symmetry, and an axis. This does not mean that all centers are perfectly symmetrical. But when an asymmetrical situation occurs, the centering process will generally try to construct the asymmetrical thing, or center, as a product of simpler centers which are themselves locally symmetrical. It does not permit random asymmetrical arrangements.

7.3. A center applies as much to space as to solid objects and buildings. Each center is thus a whole, which is made of subsidiary wholes.

7.4. When we look at a center, we see that the following rules apply:

   a. It is whole in itself, in an obvious, relaxed way, with its own symmetries.

   b. Its main parts are themselves also whole, and have their own symmetries.

   c. The space or buildings next to it, in so far as they are themselves whole, have their own symmetry.

   d. The whole is always part of some still larger whole, which is itself a center, possessing certain symmetries.

7.5 Growth and symmetry. In the process of growth, it is rarely possible for a center to be perfectly symmetrical. In fact, as the world where the centers are growing develops, it contains more and more asymmetries, induced by a succession of necessary accidents. Sometimes these existing geometrical contexts are extremely peculiar (as is true on our site in San Francisco, with freeways, Hills Brothers coffee factory, etc. all placed in such a way as to create very complex order).

The main thing which happens, then, in the process of centering, is that each new center endeavors to introduce symmetry into this field . . . *but always fails.*

This is because a naive insertion of a symmetrical object is always dead, because it is unrelated to the complex asymmetries around it. A thing which struggles to be related to the complex field around it, which tries to unite it, to make it whole, will always be almost symmetrical, but not quite . . . *not* as a result of an *intention* to be like this, but because this is the *inevitable* outcome of an effort to be *true.*

One of the reasons we can always recognize a real structure of centers as fast as we do is that we can always detect the truth in the balance of symmetry and asymmetry, even when we do not know what is going on "functionally."

Thus, we may see the creation of the field of centers, as the creation of a loosely connected system of local symmetries, always relaxed, always allowing necessity to guide it, in such a way as to produce the deepest possible structure of centers, at every scale.

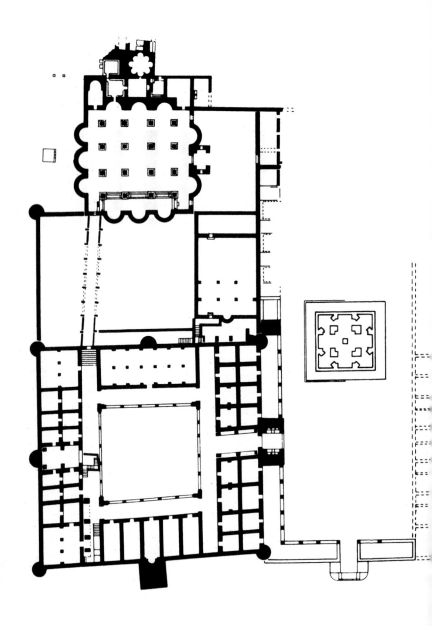

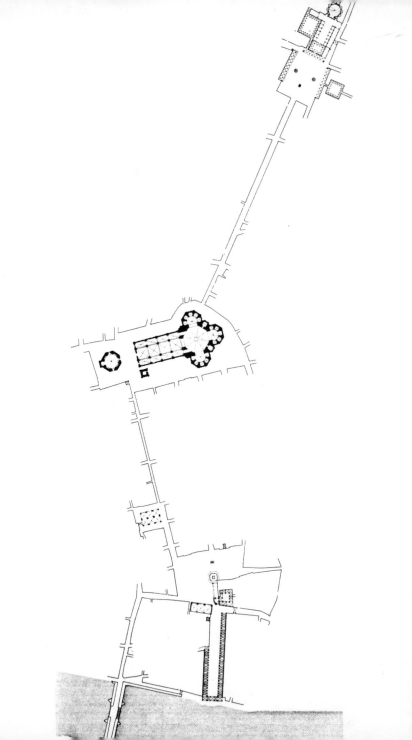

Students were somewhat slow to understand the principle of creating centers. The best examples therefore came relatively late in the simulation.

Among middle-sized centers, the library is a beautiful example (p. 218). Also the small pier (p. 208).

Among the largest centers, the bandstand was helpful, in being a small center which helped to fix a very large one (p. 200). And the central courtyard of the theater, as a center, itself surrounded by the arcade which is made up of smaller centers, but in turn helping to fix the largest center in the main square, was another very good example.

Among very small centers, we may mention the two fountains (pp. 136 and 230), and the row of bollards along the water (p. 222).

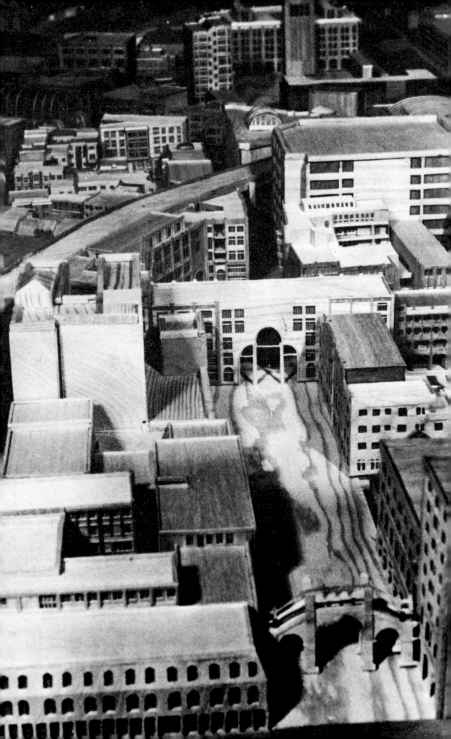

PART TWO

EXPERIMENT

Part of the completed project

We now present the main experiment itself. The experiment consists of a simulated process of urban growth, carried out by about twenty people. The simulation is entirely based on the single rule we have presented, and on the seven rules which embody it.

For the simulation, we chose a part of the San Francisco waterfront, which was destined for development in the near future. It is an area just north of the Bay Bridge, and has a total of about 30 acres. It includes several existing streets, three piers, the Hills Brothers coffee factory, and various other existing buildings, including a nightclub, an old YMCA and other warehouses and factories.

The simulation itself consists of about 90 development projects which were completed in this area, over a period of about five years.

In order to do the simulation, we first made a physical model of the whole project area at a scale of $1/32$ inch to 1 foot, with detailed models of the Bay Bridge, waterfront, streets, sidewalks, freeways, and all nearby buildings.

We thus had, in front of us, a full-scale model of the area, at all times. It was a beautiful model, carefully made, in unpainted hardwood.

Each new step in the development was always represented by the addition of some physical piece, to the overall growing model . . . just like construction in a real town. Sometimes the piece was a large piece, representing a large building complex. At other times it might be a small piece, representing a seat, or a row of bollards.

Thus, those of us who took part in the simulation had in front of us, all the time, a physical and three-dimensional model of the waterfront project area.

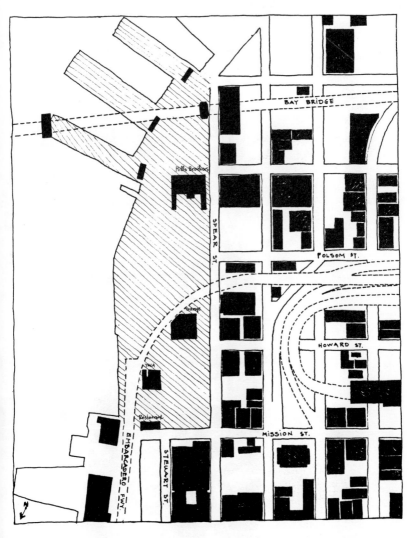

The area to be developed

Map of the completed project

EXPERIMENT

This model was our world, our reality.

In our simulation, the actual projects were created by eighteen graduate students, who "represented" developers and community groups. The developers and community groups were assumed to be building new projects, . . . prompted to do so by the dynamic development of the area.

In order to do enough projects for the whole simulation, each student had to do about six projects. However, the fact that each person did several projects had no meaning for the simulation. It was simply for experimental convenience, and we should look at the 90 projects which these eighteen students created, as if they had been created by 90 different individuals.

Since one of the rules in the process (Rule 1) gives a size distribution for development projects, the 90 projects had to fall into three broad categories: large, medium, and small, in about equal numbers. We therefore asked each student to do two large, two medium, and two small projects.

The original authors of the experiment, Chris Alexander and Ingrid King (together with Howard Davis, who helped us) took the role, in the simulation, of the committee responsible for checking and administering the growth process.

We have not specified the manner in which such a committee might be formed, or might function, in a real city. However, we can say that it would act, in a manner roughly similar to a typical planning commission, or planning authority.

There is a further aspect of the simulation, which does not correspond to real world effects. The simulation was carried out as part of the graduate program at the University of California, Berkeley. As a result, it was our task to teach students. The students who took part in this simulation, were therefore involved in *all* discussions, about every project.

As a result, there came about a considerable amount of unspoken coherence in the project, which arose from people's mutual understanding of what we were trying to accomplish.

EXPERIMENT

This phenomenon became more and more marked . . . and in the last stages of development, the students were able to function almost entirely without guidance from the committee, since the eight rules had been completely absorbed and understood.

Of course, in a real city, according to present-day development procedures, the 90 individuals creating the 90 projects would *not* communicate, and there would not, therefore, be any gradual growth of unspoken coherence.

However, it is possible to imagine a new kind of urban process, in which the various individuals and developers who take part in the creation of a given area *are* encouraged to communicate in a similar manner, through new rules, or new social systems.

The two persons who emerged as "leaders" of the student group . . . and who might, in a real world situation, also arise as natural community leaders in such a situation, are our two co-authors: Hajo Neis and Artemis Anninou.

It is largely as a result of their efforts, and persistence, that this book has been completed and brought to publication.

What happened, concretely? Each student who took part in the simulation was asked to undertake six projects, during the course of the work. Of these six projects, two had to be large, two medium, and two small.

There was no prearranged sequence of projects. Instead,

110

students were asked to examine the conditions of the area, at each moment of its development, and were asked to propose projects, whenever they felt stimulated to do so by the needs—as they saw them—of the emerging whole.

When they proposed a project, the development committee (CA,IK,HD), would examine the proposal, to see if it met the seven rules. If it did so, the project was formally accepted.

If the project was not accepted, it was sometimes sent back for modification, so that it might better conform to the rules. Other projects were discouraged entirely, as being too far from the rules to be potentially viable, even with changes.

The process of discussion by the committee, was the process by which the students learned the seven rules. Although there was a didactic function in this process, which belonged to the university, not to the simulation . . . there would also be a closely similar process, in a real city, as different developers and individuals learned to grasp these seven rules, and to put forward projects which follow these rules.

Once a proposed project had been accepted, it was then entered on a large sheet, or log . . . even in its rough state . . . so that other participants knew what was coming.

The student who proposed it, then went through a process of design development, to give it final shape . . . and finally built a model, and placed the model on the overall model of the project area.

This process, like a real process of development and construction, took time.

In the interim, other members of the community, knew roughly what was coming, since a very crude sketch, and cardboard model of the future building, was placed on the model, to indicate future construction.

This was then replaced, when the project was complete, by a perfect hardwood model, which represented the completion of the real construction project.

The model was thus, at all times, in a continual state of development, with some new projects in a partial stage, some in the stage of cardboard models, and some in a completed state. In this sense, the model seemed, at all times, like a real city in the process of development . . . with new projects, proposed projects, half-completed projects, and new buildings, all intermingled to form the actual fabric of the city at any given moment.

We shall now describe the actual unfolding of the project, step by step, as these 90 projects were created, one by one.

 othe ⁜ othe

We began with the virgin site. At this stage there were already various old buildings in different places. The overhead freeway passed through the project area, curving gently. There was an abandoned chocolate factory, towards the south, waiting for redevelopment. The waterfront had an existing highway, little used, running along it. Warehouses and piers stretched out into the water, at the southern end, under the Bay Bridge, and beyond.

Now we had to decide what to do first.

EXPERIMENT

PROJECT 1: THE GATEWAY

Of course, the most natural first question was: How shall we enter the site? What is its entrance?

Since the problem was fundamental, the committee went to visit the site, with all the students, to decide which general area seemed most right, the right place to start development.

The natural entrance to the site is from Mission Street, at the northern end of the site. We went to the site and walked and walked. The northern spot seemed the most

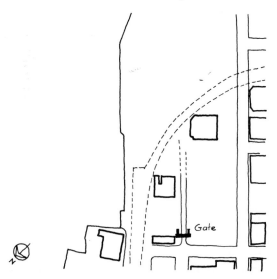

natural. Next to it is a row of old bars, Mulligan's jazz club . . . old brick buildings, with a lot of character. And west of them, the post office.

This decision . . . to start at the northern end . . . was then formally announced by the committee, with an invitation for projects that would enhance the entrance, and create it strongly and dramatically.

The first idea of what to do, came from Leslie Moldow, with a vision of a gate: a narrow, high gateway, arching

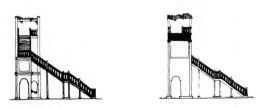

The gate elevations and section

The entrance gateway

over the street, with stairs. This gate would form the entrance to the project. It was to be non-revenue-producing, and would be built with public money.

The committee approved the general idea of the gateway. Soon afterward, the backers of the project put forward a detailed design for the gate. It was built a short time later.

COMMENTARY ON LARGER WHOLES

The gate which has been built does more than merely form a gateway. It creates the sense of a whole street which is to follow it.

Thus, the small act of building the gate, not only creates certain local wholes around the gate itself, but also hints at the formation of a much larger whole: namely the entire 300 feet of Steuart Street to the south.

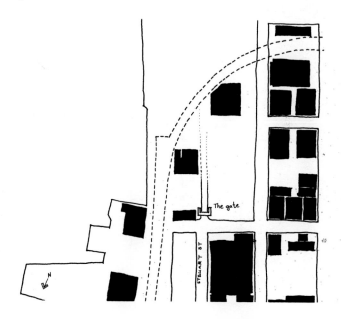

At this stage, there was a discussion of the character of this street beyond the gate, the portion of Steuart Street between the gate and the freeway.

We agreed that this street would be a mall for both cars and pedestrians. Making it exclusively pedestrian seemed too remote from city life, and too destructive to its function as a main entrance to the site. At the same time, in order to make sure that it had a strong pedestrian character, we agreed that it would be given very wide sidewalks . . . each sidewalk as wide as the central street itself . . . and a very narrow vehicular pavement on which cars would be forced to drive slowly.

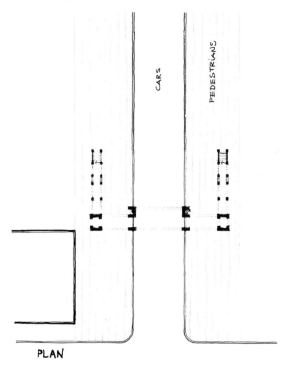

PLAN

EXPERIMENT

There was, then, general agreement that future buildings and projects would do what they could to create this mall, and to give it the right character. However, our agreement did not take the form of any definite map or plan, since we wanted the mall to develop under the impetus of its own increments. We merely agreed to watch it carefully to protect its character as it emerged.

PROJECT 2: THE HOTEL

According to the rules (especially Rule 2) the next project must do something to enhance this whole, enlarge it, strengthen it, and heal it. There was some discussion of this point, between the committee and the participants.

In response to this discussion, Jim McLane then proposed to build a hotel, next to the gate. The idea was that the volume of the hotel would begin to shape a pedestrian street behind the gate. The hotel was to be financed privately.

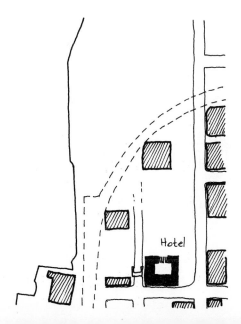

Hotel

EXPERIMENT

The committee accepted the proposal, and Mr. McLane
carried out the details of the building as shown here:

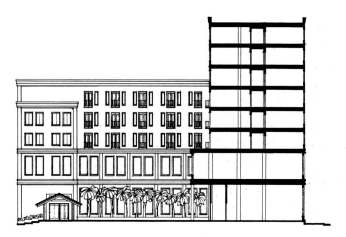

Hotel section looking southwest

Northeast elevation

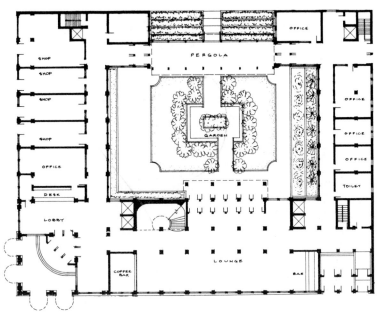

Hotel ground floor plan

Entrance elevation

One of the most important and beautiful aspects of the hotel was the fact that Mr. McLane proposed, and built, a small garden at the back of the hotel, to serve the guests. The idea was that this small garden would later open out into a larger and more public garden, which would be built at some time in the future.

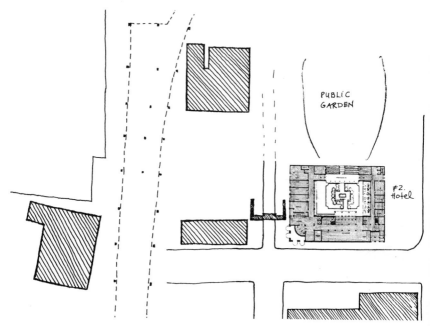

Thus, once again, a small whole, contained the seed of a larger, imagined whole which was to come later. This idea was quickly made public and shared by all the participants in the project, so that we knew (collectively) that efforts should be made to try to bring this imagined public garden into existence. (This kind of procedure, incidentally, was typical, and essential, throughout the project . . . someone would have a vague idea of a public entity that needed to be created, and individual projects were then encouraged to help, by small steps, to create the larger entity, cooperatively).

PROJECT 3: THE CAFE

The first project to help bring the idea of the garden into existence was the café.

It is placed in such a way that it helps to extend (and form) the mall on its front side . . . and the garden along the back. It is thus a very useful, and beautifully placed project, since it helps to make the spaces all around it whole.

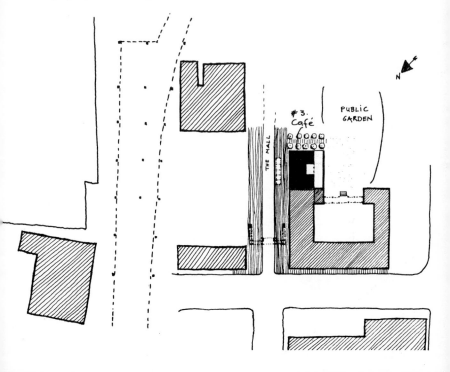

EXPERIMENT

The café was put forward by Martine Weissmann. She described her vision of the café like this: "When you pass through the gate, on your right you see a three-storey café. The front of the café faces the busy pedestrian sidewalk. The back has a sunny terrace which opens onto a public garden."

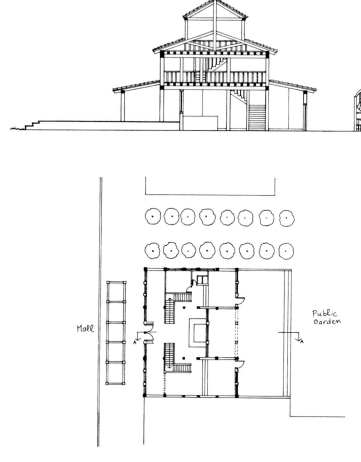

Cafe ground floor plan and section

EXPERIMENT

Martine Weissmann brought this idea forward as a private person. She built and financed the café privately.

PROJECT 4: MARKET AND FISHING PIER

At the same time, opposite the café, on the other side of the mall, another structure emerged as a result of Hubert Froyen's vision: "Standing between the YMCA and the French restaurant, looking towards the water, I see a beautiful dome in front of the freeway, and under it, a tunnel passing through the freeway leading to the other side. At the end of the tunnel, I see a wooden pier, and part of the Bay. Inside the tunnel there is light, and almost no noise. Openings in the left wall of the tunnel lead to a market. Openings in the right wall lead to another, more permanent food market. At the end of the food market, there is a fishmarket with fresh fish brought in from the fishing boats."

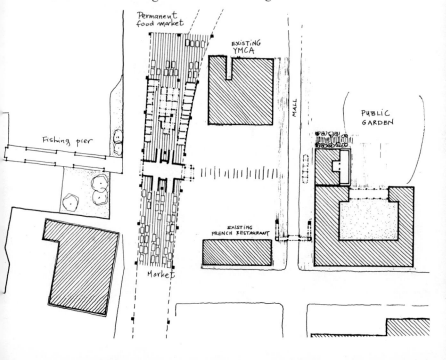

Thus, after walking through the gate, if you turn left, you walk on a not yet clearly defined path, and there you see a beautiful dome in front of the freeway. The dome leads to a market under the freeway: and that in turn leads to a fishing pier on the far side of the freeway. At Mr.

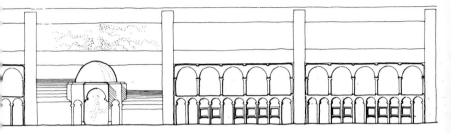

Food market southwest elevation

Froyen's suggestion, the market and fishing pier were to be financed by a combination of public and private funds.

This project ties together the developing mall with the water, and so begins to heal the waterfront. Also, by creating a market under the freeway, it has the effect of mending the dangerous and unpleasant under-freeway area.

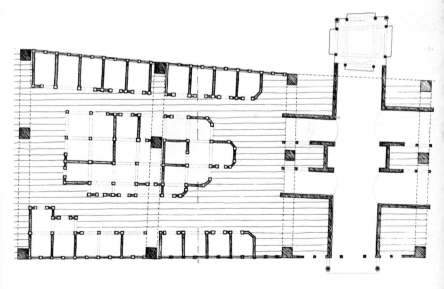

Food market and tunnel plan

EXPERIMENT

PROJECT 5: COMMUNITY BANK

Next, it was time to form the mall more clearly. Discussion among various developers, and members of the committee, had shown that the mall itself was still vague and ambiguous in certain respects. We didn't know how long it was, where it would end, and where it would lead to.

As a result of these discussions, the committee invited proposals which would help to give the mall a definite boundary and shape.

The first proposal which struck a chord was one made by a group of citizens headed by Artemis Anninou, for a community bank. The bank is a group of three buildings, built around a square. This square was to form the endpoint of the Steuart Street mall.

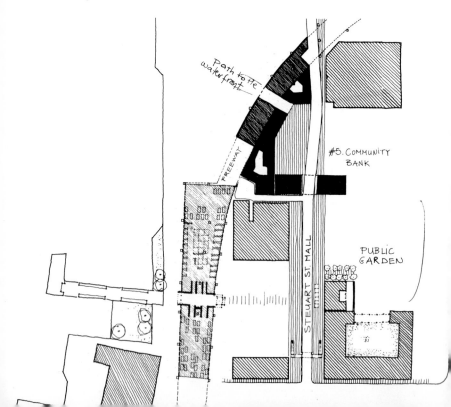

At the end of the street, where the street enters the square, there was to be a gateway . . . and there was to be a second gateway, on the far side of the square, where the path passes under the freeway, and leads towards the water.

In this example, we see how the theory of centers and the one rule really work. We have the unfinished state, before the proposal, and we then have the finished state, after the proposal, which is formed by a rather extensive system of centers, that closes, and completes the situation, and also opens out its arms towards possible future development beyond.

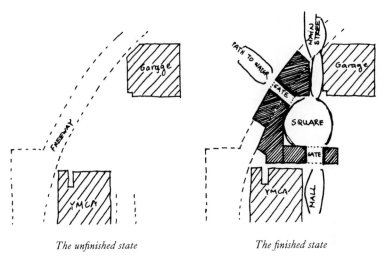

The unfinished state   *The finished state*

In order to make this system of centers effective, and coherent, it is also necessary—as we shall see later—for a variety of minor centers to embellish the whole, and to bring it to life. These centers will include a fountain and a kiosk (project 11).

EXPERIMENT

The whole project is an excellent example of the way that a project is defined, not merely by its own functional needs, but by the role it has to play in helping to heal the environment around it. It gets its shape mainly from the configurations which arise from the attempt to play this healing role.

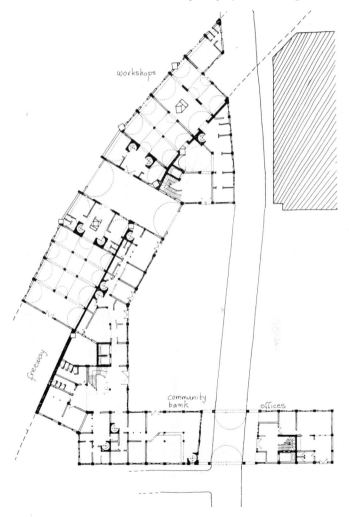

Community bank ground floor plan

EXPERIMENT

The next four projects were large ones, which continued to fill out the structures which had been defined so far:

6: BUILDING COMPLEX

7: APARTMENT BUILDING

8: APARTMENT BUILDING

9: PARKING GARAGE AND APARTMENTS

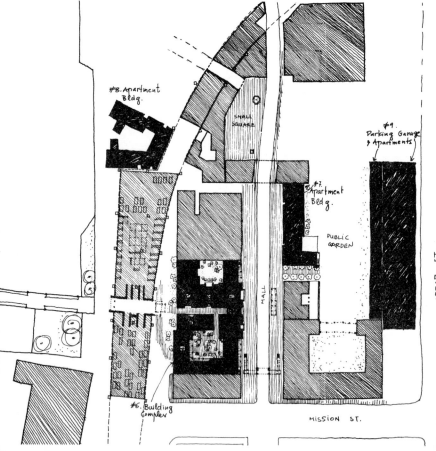

Each of these projects simply built a large, commercially viable building, in a position which clearly helped to contain the public elements which had been begun. The building complex and two apartment buildings all shaped the mall. The building complex also helped to complete the small path to the water. And the parking garage and apartment building on the west, helped to contain the public garden. The parking structure was required, according to the details of Rule 4, to provide the amount of parking needed to support the structures built so far.

Lobby of building complex

EXPERIMENT

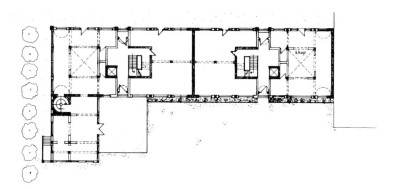

Apartment building #7, northeast elevation and ground floor plan

10: HEDGES AND PAVING

By now the mall, or street, had received a definite character. Its function was clear. Its ends had been defined. Its
edges had been defined.

In order to solidify it, and to give it its final form, Mr.
Takeshi Kimura, came forward to propose the details of

134

paving and planting which would set its character. These details were to be paid for by public works.

He showed us a vision of several parallel bands: paving stones, a long continuous bench, a hedge, and a trench filled with gravel. These bands were to contain and hold together the wide sidewalks and the street, by making a series of boundaries between pedestrians and cars.

At one point, there was even a "rest house" . . . a tiny pavilion built between the seats and hedges, where a person could sit and wait in the shade.

It made a very quiet street.

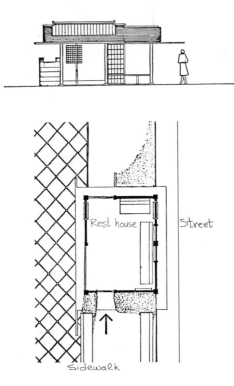

Rest house elevation and plan

EXPERIMENT

11: FOUNTAIN AND KIOSK

Shortly afterward, Ms. Shohreh Daemi brought us her vision of the fountain in the square. When she showed it to us, she included a small kiosk, thus giving the square two smaller centers, not one, to balance its complicated shape.

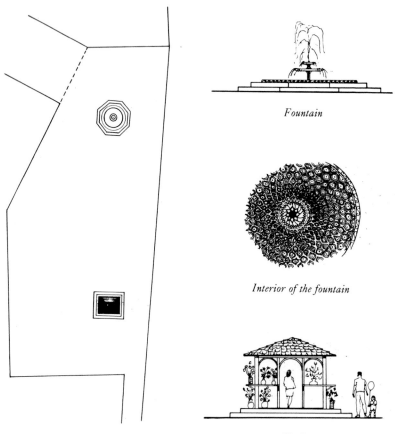

Fountain

Interior of the fountain

Plan of the square with kiosk and fountain

Kiosk

12: EDUCATIONAL CENTER

This was the last increment to complete the south-west side of the square.

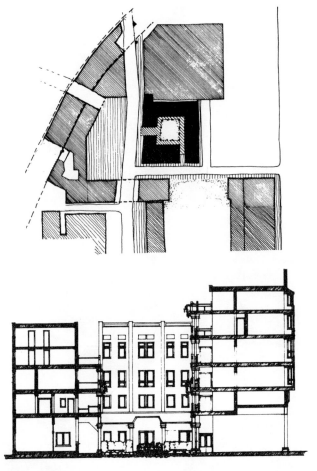

Educational center site plan and section through courtyard

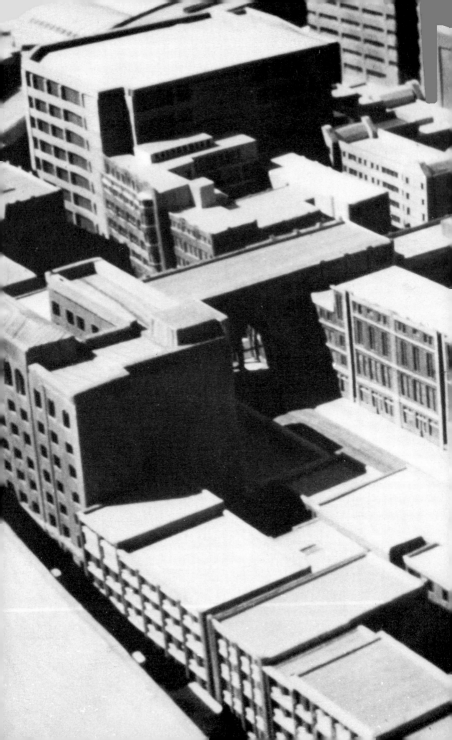

EXPERIMENT

COMMENTARY ON EMERGING WHOLES

So far the development of the whole project had been piece-meal, without any clear relationship to any ultimate overall center of the project.

At this stage it is necessary to explain something that had happened much earlier in the life of the committee. At a much earlier stage, the committee and all the developers together, visited the project site.

We agreed, after some time, that the major center of the project would be a big square roughly in the middle, next to the water, and we agreed, also, that it would have to face a very specific direction . . . almost facing the Bay Bridge and the south sun, but slightly to the left of it, looking at the main body of water of the Bay.

We all felt that this location, and this axis, were created by the site itself. They could be strongly felt by everyone.

In this sense then, all the development which had happened so far, was done, with the knowledge that sooner or later the development would reach the middle, and would then have to generate a coherent square in this middle. We might say that the mall, and street, and garden built so far, were merely the preparatory or peripheral structures, which had begun to form a gradient towards this ultimate greater center . . . even though the greater center so far existed only in our imaginations, and had never been given any concrete form at all . . . except for the two points already mentioned: its location and its orientation.

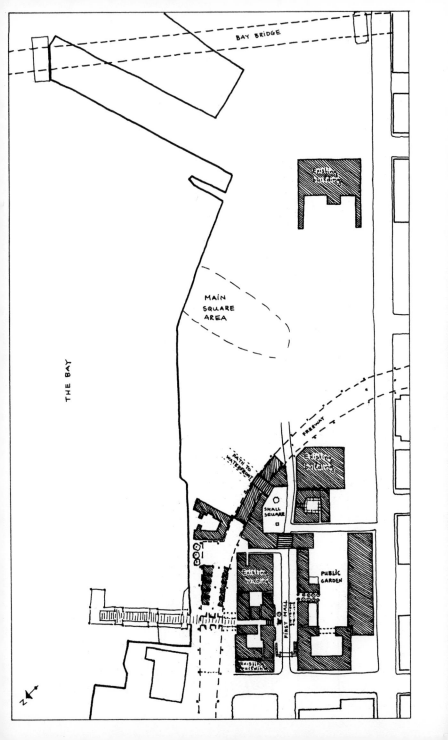

13: BATH

At this stage a major event took place.

During earlier experiments, we had noticed that often during the development process, a new whole was created,

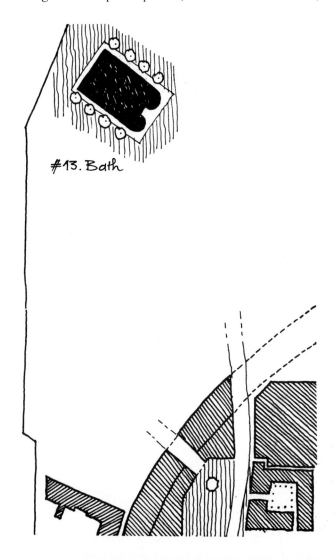

#13. Bath

not by a continuous formation of structures touching previous ones, but by a jump into unexplored territory where something is done to begin the formation of an entirely new center. We called this process "leapfrogging."

So far, all the projects had grown mainly by small steps, each one very close to the previous ones. Now, we had an extraordinary jump . . . a leapfrog . . . out into the very middle of the project area.

Carsten Schmunk, came to us with a proposal for a bath house near the water. He described a vision of a kind of crystal palace, a steel and glass structure, right by the water.

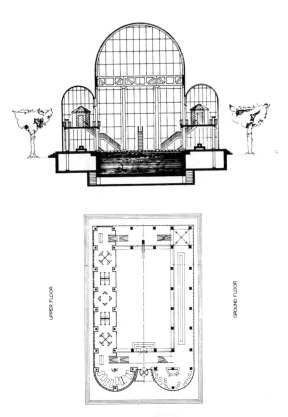

Bath section and plans

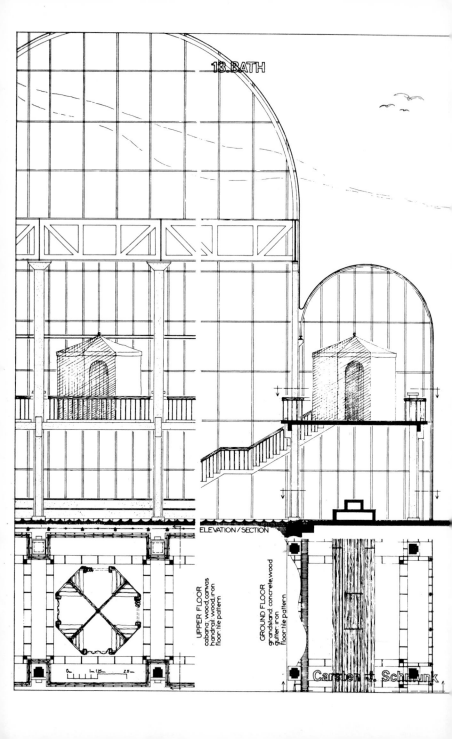

13.BATH

ELEVATION / SECTION

UPPER FLOOR
cabana; wood, canvas
handrail: wood, iron
floor: tile pattern

GROUND FLOOR
grandstand: concrete, wood
gutter: iron
floor: tile pattern

Carsten J. Schmuck

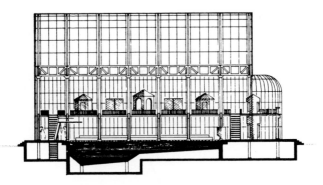

Longitudinal section

The vision was not directly related to the idea of a square in the middle of the project. At the time of its construction it was merely intended to "initiate a center in the emerging community."

But, as it turned out, the vision of the bathhouse was so strong, and captured everyone's imagination to such a degree, that it naturally became the kernel of the great central square . . . and many, many projects followed, placing themselves around it to form the square in the years after its construction.

14: TREES ALONG WATER

Imagine the site, in its state after the bathhouse is built. A whole has been created in the middle of a vacuum. Now certain actions had to be taken to unite this new whole with the previous developments, so that the empty space between could also become whole.

EXPERIMENT

First, one of the small-scale actions required by Rule 1 . . . simply planting trees. Hye Myoung Kim came forward with a vision of trees along the water. . . . The trees were placed in a line along the waterfront, so that the bath became connected physically to the market and the pier built earlier. This made the whole stretch of waterfront from the market to the bath a single thing.

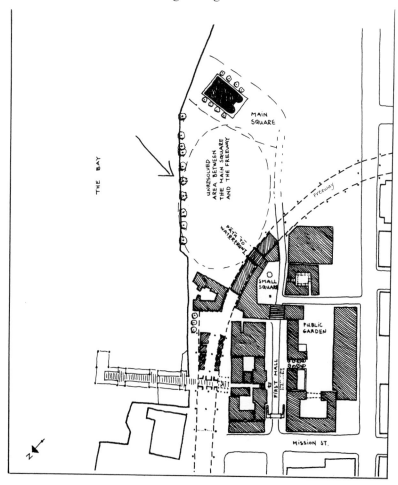

Still, however, there was a gap of some kind, a gaping hole, a lack of connection in the tissue. It is easy to see this gap on the diagram opposite. The path from the mall passes under the curve of the freeway . . . but where does it go? The trees on the waterfront lead along the water . . . but where is there a place to stop? The area between the freeway and the bath must be developed . . . but what is its natural center?

Various proposals were made, to solve the problem . . . but none of them seemed right or interesting. The first thing that we heard about, that had the quality of truly filling this gap, a vision of some weight, was the proposal made by Hajo Neis.

15: CHURCH

He had a vision of a church at the connecting point between the path coming from the mall and the waterfront.

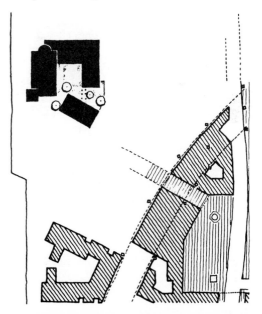

The church was to be right on the water, with its own cloister and seminary.

It has a major church hall parallel to the waterfront, with a tower at its front corner.

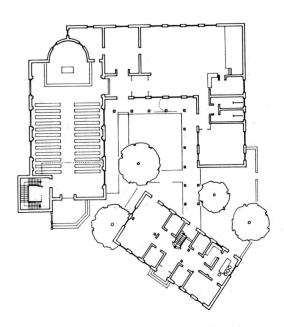

Church northwest elevation and ground floor plan

EXPERIMENT

COMMENTARY ON FORMATION OF LARGER
WHOLES

At this stage, the area between the bathhouse and the previous development, was beginning to be coherent.

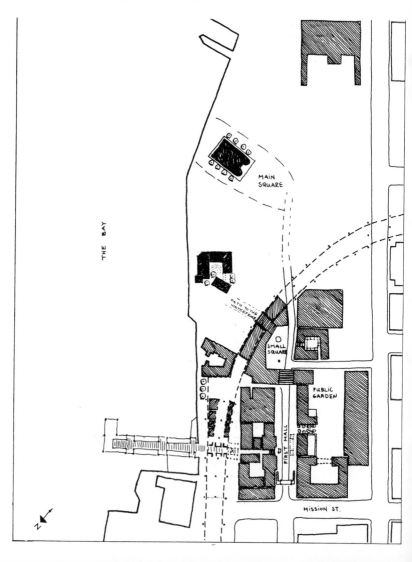

Since this large problem had been solved, it was natural now for people to relax a little, from the arduous tasks of staking out the global character of what was going to happen, and to go back and fill in some details in the earlier structure.

At this stage, therefore, two projects were built which completed the public garden, started a long time earlier. This delayed process was typical. The garden had first been hinted at at the very beginning, in project 2. It was then strongly developed by the café. Later its shape was thoroughly defined by the parking structure and apartments on the east and west.

Now, much later, the final steps were taken to complete this garden.

16: CONDOMINIUM WITH A KINDERGARTEN
18: GARDEN WITH PAGODA

The first step, project 16, was a proposal made by a developer, Mr. Mahn Oh, for a condominium. This condominium was to close the garden on the south side, and

Condominium with kindergarten

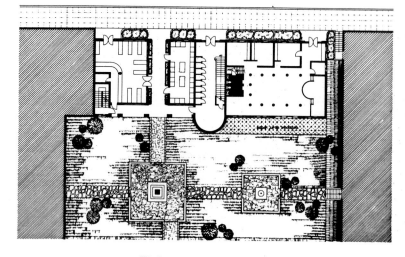

Kindergarten ground floor plan

was to contain a kindergarten on the ground floor, so that the children could go directly into the garden.

The second stage, more in the nature of a vision, also came from Mahn Oh. Originally born in South Korea, Mr. Oh wanted to make a garden with a strongly Korean character. He proposed to pay for this garden privately, as a gift to the city.

The garden was to include a trellised walk, crossing the

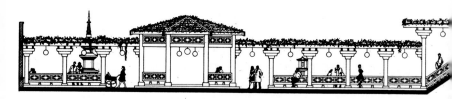

Trellised walk in the garden

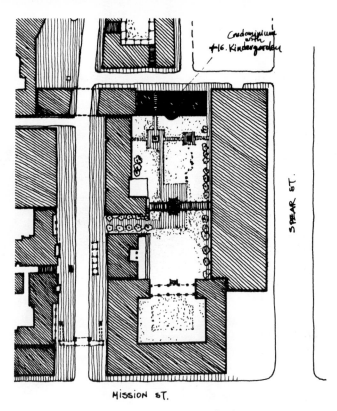

The public garden as completed

garden at the point where it connected to the mall . . . and
a pagoda, placed in the area outside the kindergarten.

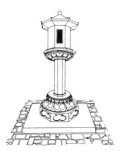

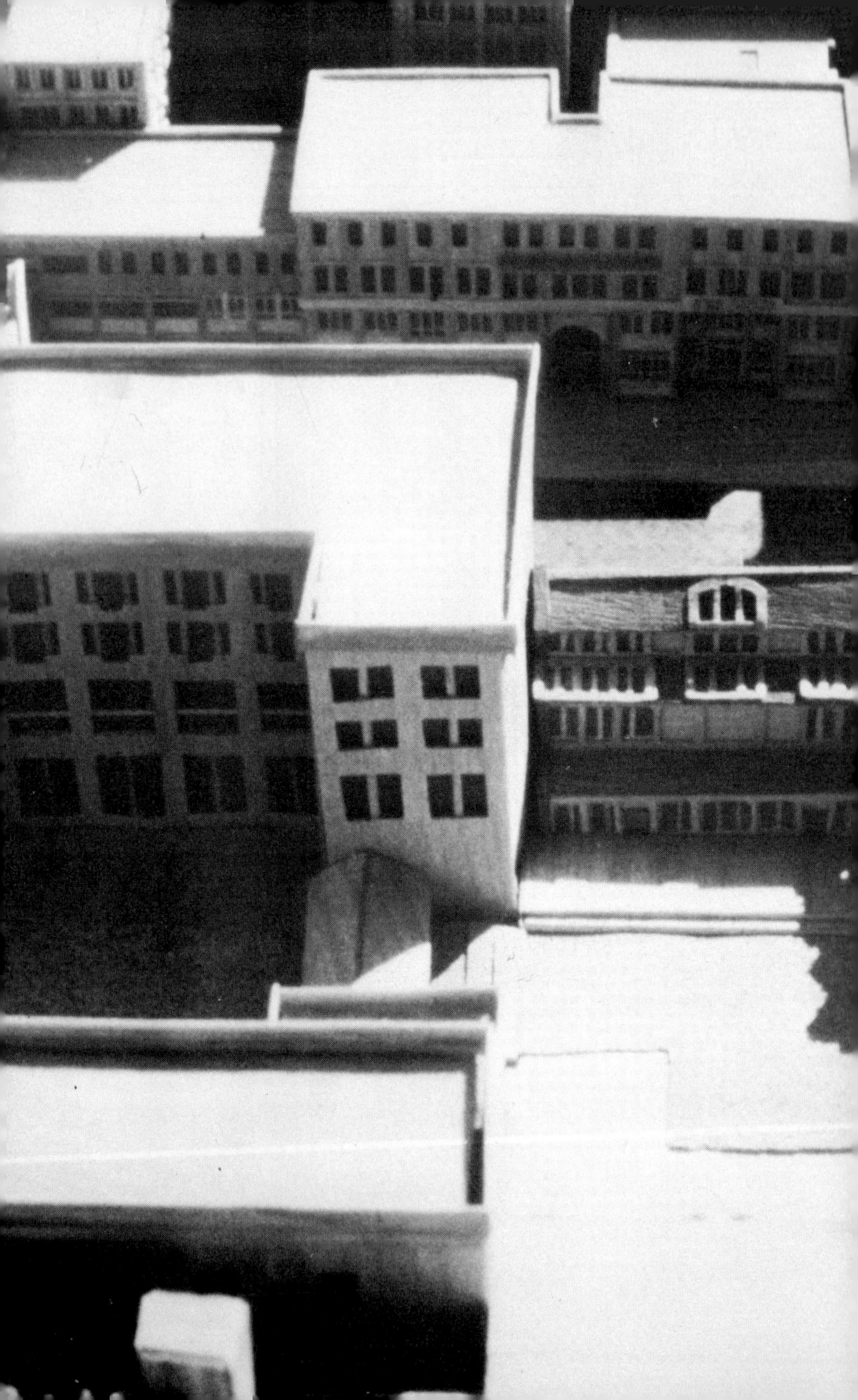

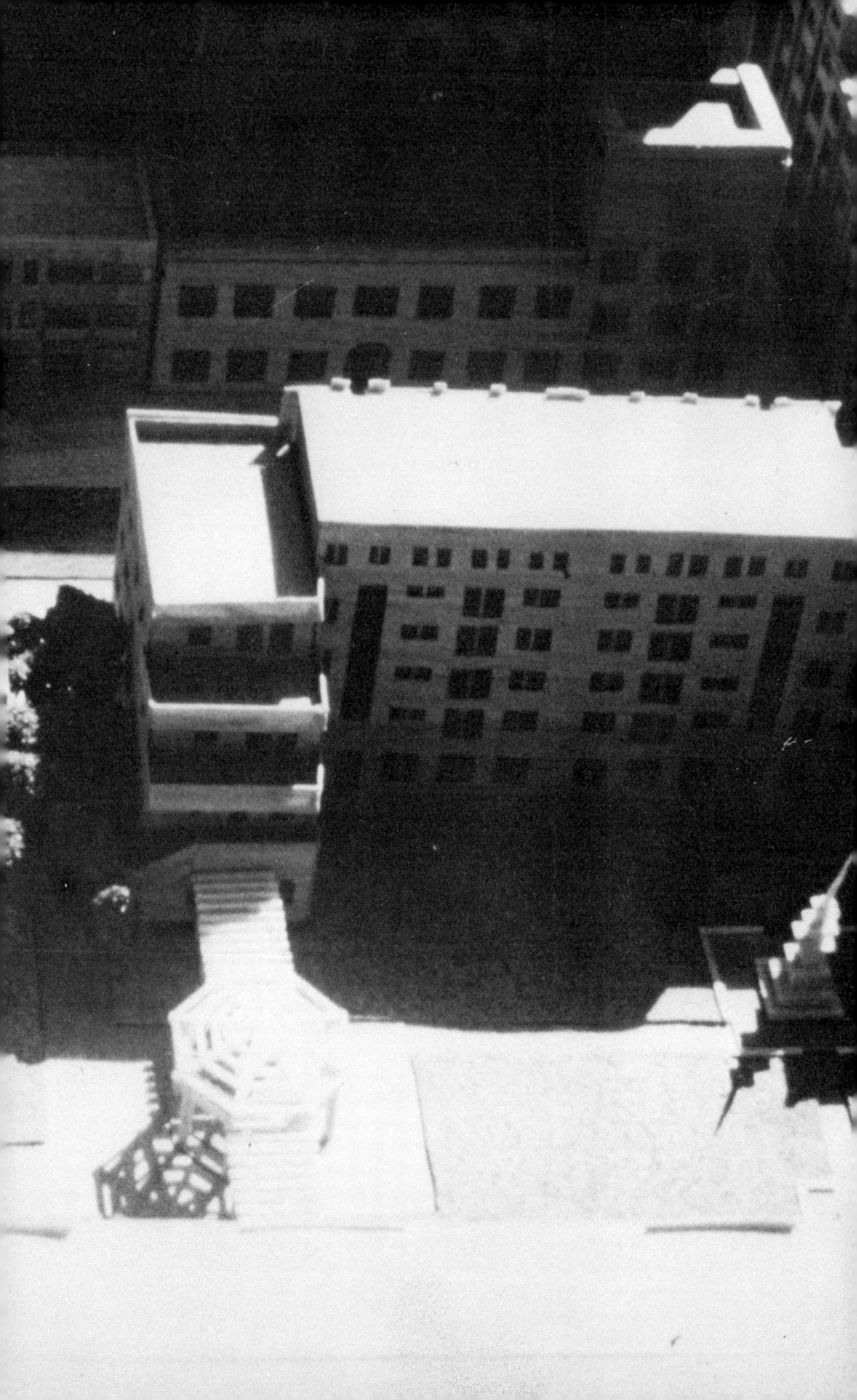

EXPERIMENT

COMMENTARY

At this stage, various other minor items of repair were done. The next five projects all simply helped to establish structures which had already been created . . . and merely needed to be filled in by development.

19: RESIDENTIAL BUILDING AND BAKERY

20: ROW HOUSES

21: LIGHTS

22: OFFICE BUILDING

24: A PARKING GARAGE

25: CAR REPAIR SHOP

The biggest of these projects was the residential building and bakery near the freeway. The row houses helped to create a link, already imagined earlier, between the gate through the freeway and the church. The lights helped to establish the waterfront promenade, already fixed by the planting of trees much earlier. The office building closed a gap in a corner left undeveloped at the very beginning. The parking garage filled the awkward ugly corner by the freeway with the necessary parking as dictated by Rule 4. The car repair shop filled a small odd corner under the freeway.

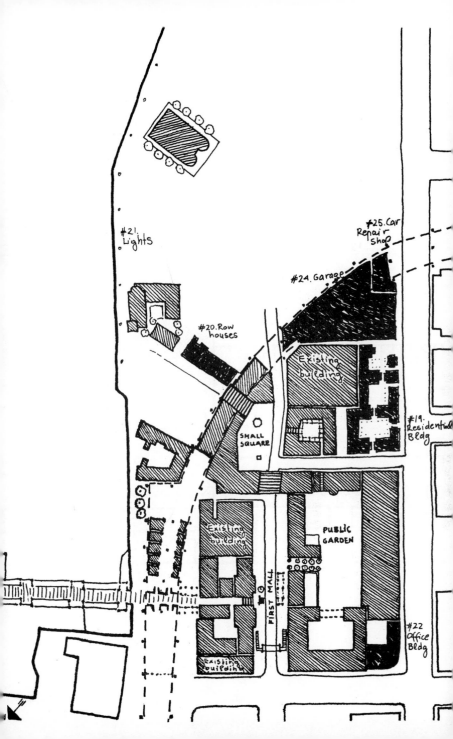

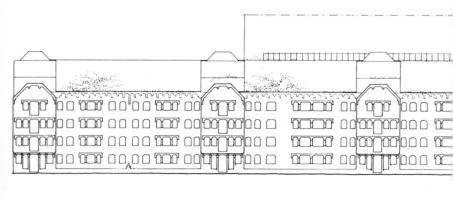

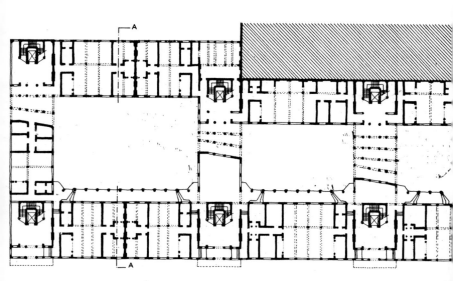

Residential buildings and bakery

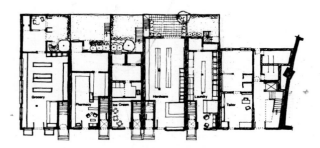

Row houses, elevation and plan

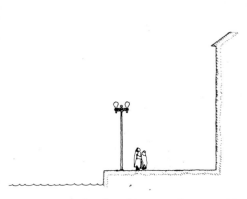

Lights along the promenade

A parking garage

Car repair shop

EXPERIMENT

COMMENTARY: THE GRID

At this stage, a danger presented itself. The path from the freeway to the church, and the row houses which help to shape this path, have the same kind of physical and geometrical character as the earlier development. It is slightly straggling, loose, and easy going.

But what was pleasant in the small area of the first part of the development around the garden and the mall, might not be at all pleasant, if continued in the much larger area which was going to be developed next. The curve of the freeway imposed an irregularity which would be hard to control. There was a real danger that there would be a randomness, a feeling of incoherence, that would be impossible to tolerate . . . and also impossible to correct, if it was not corrected early on.

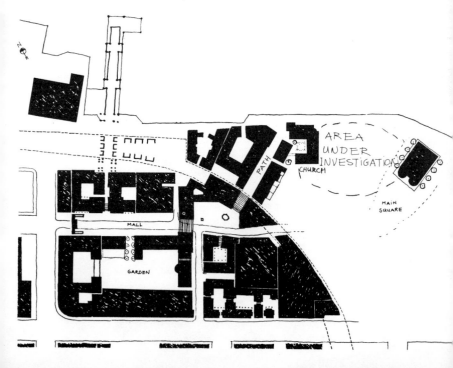

In order to make sure this didn't happen, the members of the committee now made a proposal, of a general nature: namely, that in the general area bounded by the freeway, the waterfront, and the main square, there would be a grid of tiny streets, leading to the water.

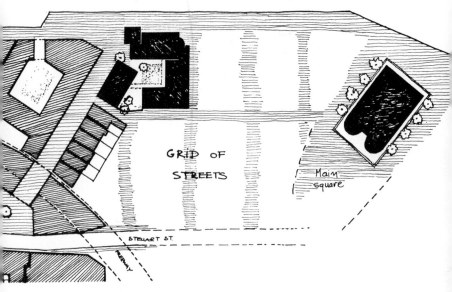

At first, this proposal caused some resistance . . . members of the class felt that it violated the spirit of the project, since it greatly resembled a master plan.

Slowly, discussion made it clear that this proposal was quite unlike a conventional master plan, since it merely identified a structure of emerging centers in a very small area . . . but by making it explicit, helped it to develop coherently.

EXPERIMENT

Thus, the grid, and its scale of very small streets and very small buildings, creates a center to support the bath house, and the coming main square, in a fashion which is consistent with the waterfront, the promenade, and the car-street which must be built further back from the water.

It is a vision of small pedestrian streets, connecting the car-street to the water, and making the walk to the water the dominant feeling of the area.

The following projects, just began to pin down the grid. They are pleasant, simple. Two buildings to fix the corner; a handrail and benches along the water to make the promenade stronger.

23: HOTEL

26: CAFE AND APARTMENTS

27: HANDRAIL AND BENCHES

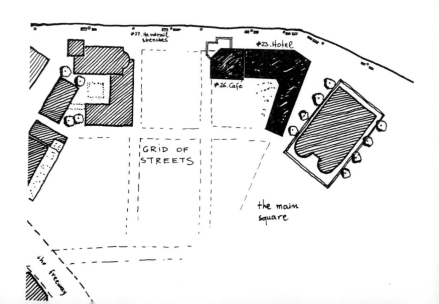

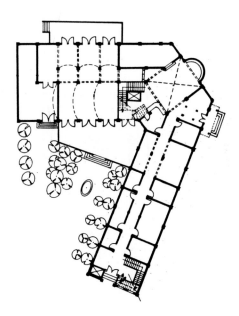

Hotel elevation and plan

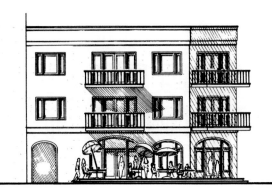

Cafe and apartments

Plan of benches along the water

Handrail and benches elevation

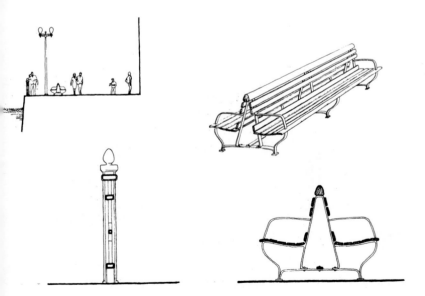

Details of handrail and bench

Then one of the most important things happened, that began to give the grid a character, a personality, that made it
more than just an abstract grid.

28: ALICE'S PARK

29: APARTMENTS

First, Alice Sung proposed a public project, a small
park on a pier jutting out into the water. This small symmetrical park was to be seen down the main street of the
grid. It would distinguish between the major and minor
grid streets going to the water. There was something clear,
simple, small, to go towards. Suddenly one had a vision of
something very definite and nice.

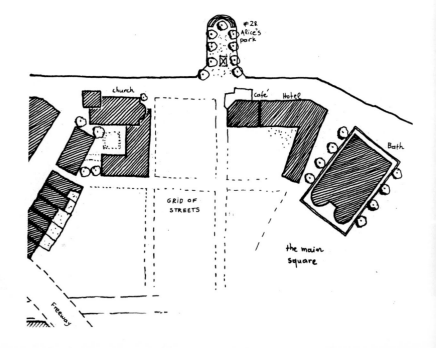

Then, shortly afterward, Ms. Sung made a second proposal . . . this time a private development, to be built along the same main street of the grid: a small apartment house.

But what was most significant, with its front wall, this apartment house became the first building to fix the actual dimension of the main grid street. She placed it in such a way as to ensure, and fix, the fact that this street was the widest one of the grid streets, and thus the "main" street. To be sure, she had first got public money for the small pier park, and had then placed a private building on this street—thus making sure of the value of her building.

But this was a small thing, compared with the fact that the grid now had a character, a spine, a personality, a center.

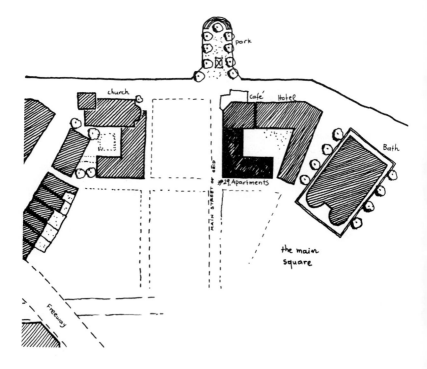

Then followed a sequence of small buildings of various types, filling out the grid:

30: ROW HOUSES

31: APARTMENT AND PUB

32: APARTMENT HOUSE

33: OFFICE AND HOUSE

34: APARTMENTS AND SHOPS

These projects were the first buildings to create the grid. Each one of them tried, in its fashion, to create a piece of the grid, at the right scale, with the right feeling.

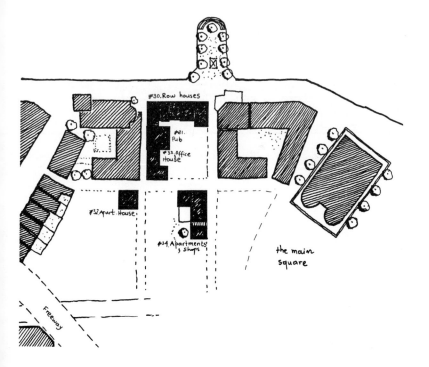

First Hye Myoung Kim built row houses along the water:

Second floor plan

Waterfront elevation

Then Carsten Schmunk built a pub with apartments over it, beginning to form the second street of the grid:

Then Takeshi Kimura built another very small apartment house:

Then James McLane built an office with a house attached to it:

Then Artemis Anninou built a group of apartments and shops:

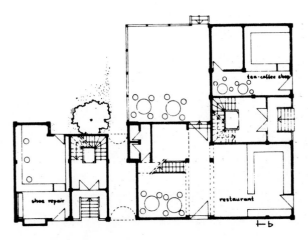

Apartments and shops, section and ground floor plan

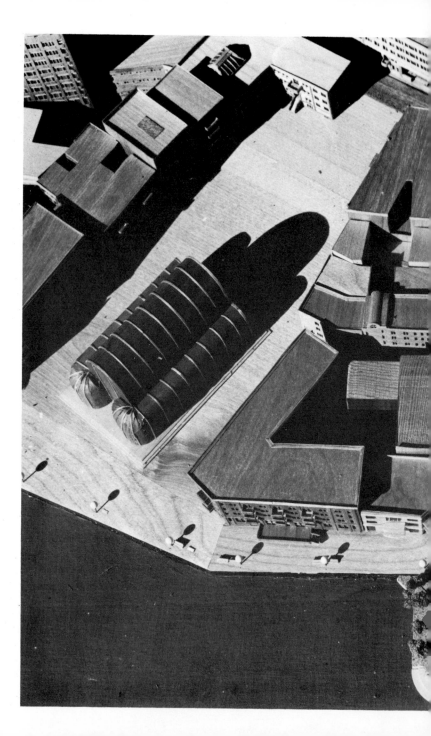

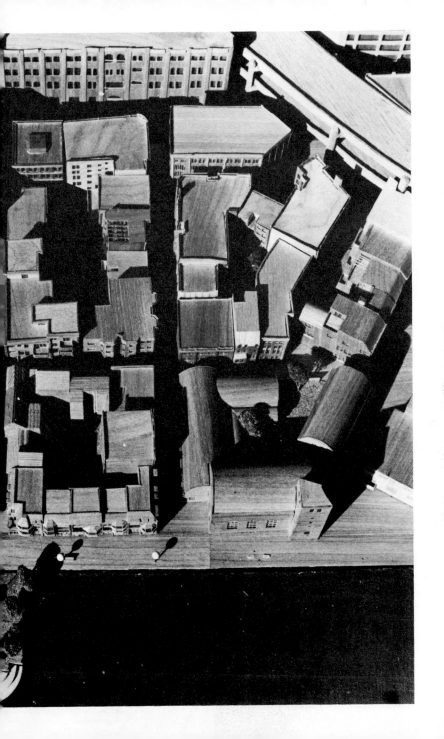

EXPERIMENT

Finally, Hajo Neis broke the sequence, with a slightly different (though related) project over on the waterfront:

35: HOUSEBOAT PIER

The pier tried to enclose the piece of water next to the grid, and give it coherent form.

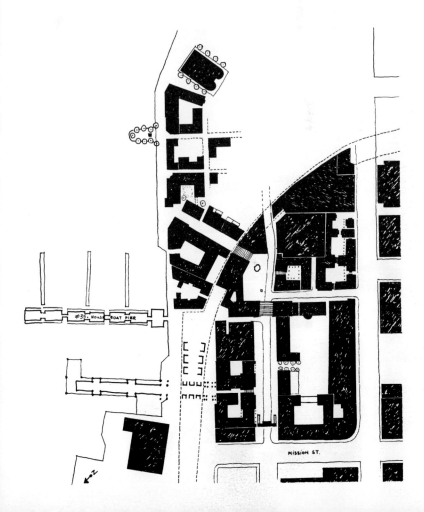

COMMENTARY ON THE GREAT SQUARE

As we explained earlier, all the participants knew, in some way, that there would be a great central square, at the middle of the project . . . and after the bathhouse was built, we knew that it would be, more or less, in the same position . . . with the bathhouse a kind of cork in its mouth where it meets the water.

Now, the growth of the grid, especially its southern edge, had begun to define the outline of the square enough so that we already had a hazy view of it, defined by the bathhouse and the edge of the grid.

However, there was still no real certainty about its shape or size.

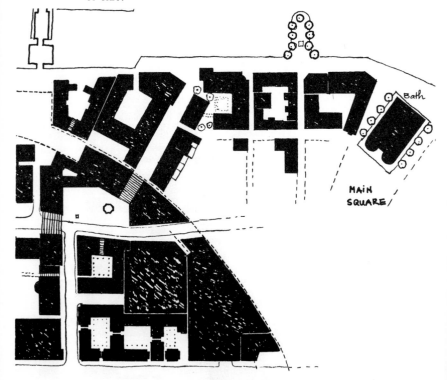

EXPERIMENT

At this stage, we felt that it was time to get this clear, since any further development without a clear sense of this problem, might unintentionally do damage, or block off possibilities.

We also agreed that the critical site, for defining the square, lay at the far end, opposite the bath. Whatever was built there would both determine the size of the square and its subtle shape. Thus the building of a project on this site was essential and crucial to the definition and success of the square.

We therefore announced, that it was now time to get a project which would do this job. Several projects were proposed. But, unfortunately, one after another we had to reject them. They were either too complex, not complex enough, too banal, not suitable in function, not spiritual enough in content, not simple enough in shape . . . in short, this was a very difficult problem indeed.

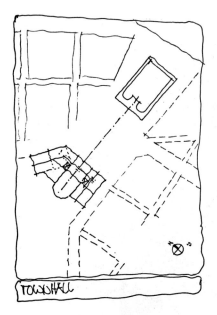

Rejected proposal

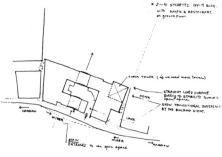

Rejected proposal

Even though they were frustrated by this situation, the participants who proposed the rejected projects, agreed, with good grace, that it was correct to reject them, and that no one had yet found anything that would make the square beautiful enough, or important enough.

Finally, the committee received a project which seemed good enough. It was, in fact, composed of two separate projects, in one:

36: THEATER AND NEWSPAPER BUILDING

Artemis Anninou described a vision of a beautiful court-yard, a kind of smaller space, surrounded by columns and arcades, several storeys high . . . and that this formal courtyard, quite perfect in shape, was to be the endpiece of the square, opening directly into the larger square, and forming its end.

The courtyard was to be the entrance, foyer, and court-yard of a theater.

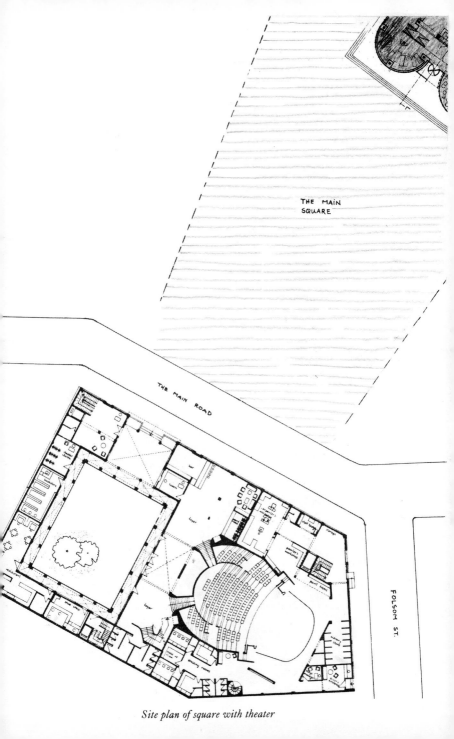

THE MAIN
SQUARE

THE MAIN ROAD

FOLSOM ST.

Site plan of square with theater

Second, we had found out, during the experiments and failed projects which preceded it, that a single building could not form the end correctly, because it always made the wrong shape for the square.

She then showed us a vision of a second building, much more mundane, but also central and public in character . . . the office of a newspaper . . . which would curl around the square, and allow cars and trucks to drive on a road between it and the theater.

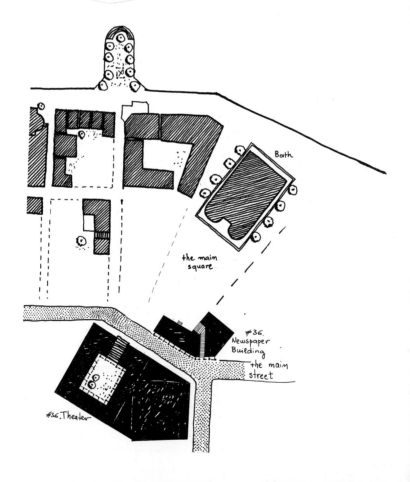

EXPERIMENT

This kind of double "end," was the most subtle way to form the square.

Newspaper building street elevation

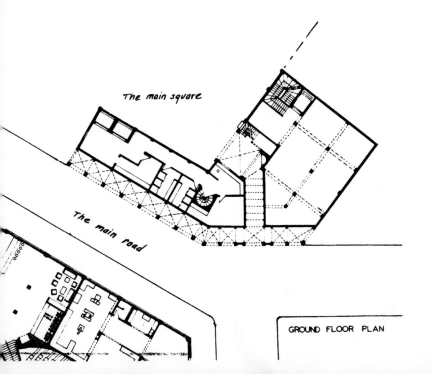

The main square

The main road

GROUND FLOOR PLAN

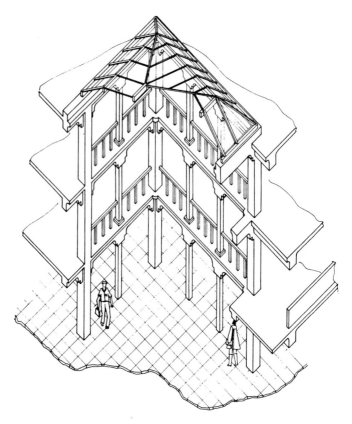

Lobby of the newspaper building

Now, with the shape of the main square clearly defined, further buildings could be added to the grid, in those positions which also helped to define and complete the shape of the square.

37: POLITICAL MEETING HALL AND APARTMENTS

41: POST OFFICE

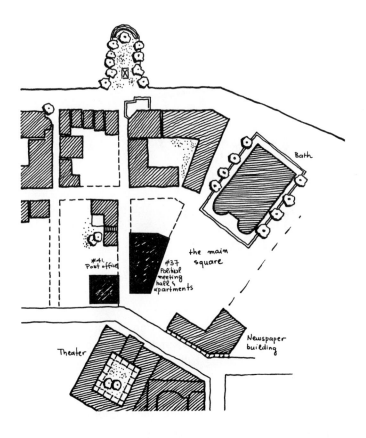

At the key corner, Martine Weissmann, the proprietor of the café near the entrance gate, now proposed to build an

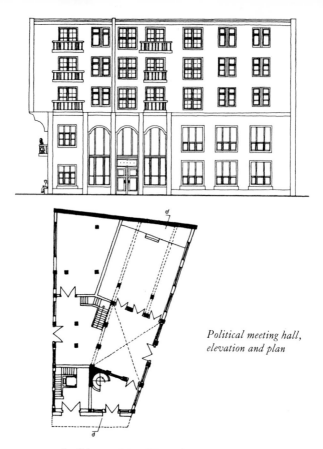

*Political meeting hall,
elevation and plan*

apartment building. Ms. Weissmann, a Parisienne with
socialist leanings, also proposed to build a privately financed political meeting hall on the ground floor and to
encourage community discussion in this hall.

Because of its location—both occupying a key position
in the grid, and helping to define the exterior envelope of
the main square—this building could not avoid a very curious exterior shape. Luckily the building got a lot of charm
from the complicated interior created by its outside shape.

188

EXPERIMENT

Ramzi Kawar proposed to build a small post office as a private development for offices, with the post office itself on the ground floor. For some reason, perhaps its simplicity, everyone remembers this building and talks about it. It became a real focus in people's minds.

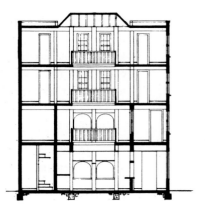

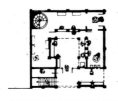

FIRST FLOOR   SECOND FLOOR   THIRD FLOOR   FOURTH FLOOR

Post office elevation,
section and floor plans

EXPERIMENT

COMMENTARY ON DEVELOPING LARGER WHOLES

At this stage, the site was more than half developed. However, there was still a complete absence of any picture of the whole structure which might emerge at the far end . . . the southern end.

This fact was translated into an experience which we might describe like this: the wholes of the northern half of the site were fairly well developed, and had a certain sense of coherence. However, at the southern end there was a gap, a lack of wholeness, and a lack of specific wholes . . . a sort of vacuum in the field of centers, which called for some new center to be created.

The next proposal created just such a center, at the southern end.

43: SHIP REPAIR

Carsten Schmunk now described to us how he saw the organic character of the waterfront maintained as an area devoted to shipping, not lost to tourism. He expressed this through his idea of transforming one of the old existing piers for a new industrial use still related to shipping:

> Pier 28 shall be devoted to maritime support industry. It is intended to install a ship repair facility, serving pleasure boats as well as commercial liners and fishing vessels. This means to provide covered working spaces, where machinery can be put up next to a berth, with storage for parts and material. This will happen in a high, well-lit hall.

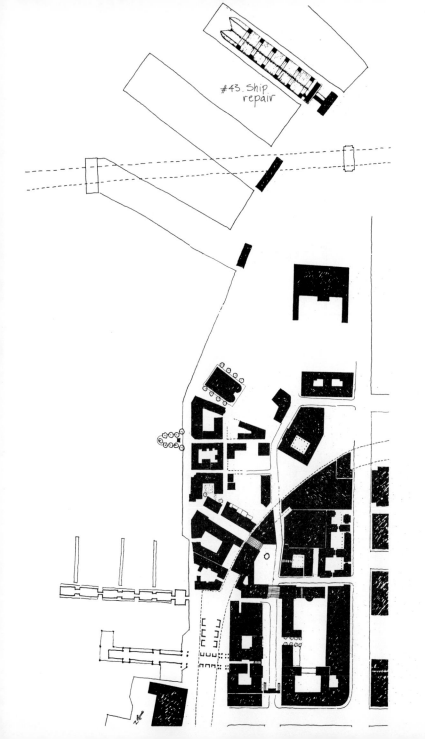

#43. Ship
repair

Furthermore a rail slip capable of hoisting up to 50-foot vessels, will be built at the end of the pier. At the other end there will be rooms for administration. The structure is rather simple like any ordinary pier shed.

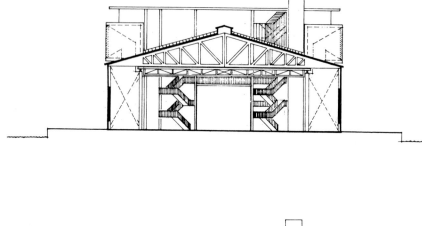

Ship repair, section and back elevation

COMMENTARY ON THE COMPLETION
OF THE GRID

Meanwhile, small buildings which filled out the grid continued to be built. The bakery, the housing for the elderly, the art gallery, and a small residence are among the most charming.

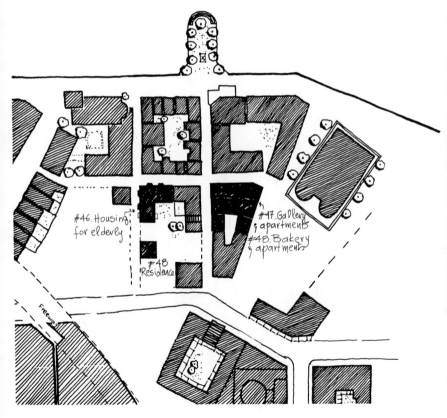

#46. Housing for elderly

#47. Gallery & apartments

#48. Bakery & apartments

#48 Residence

Freeway

44: BAKERY

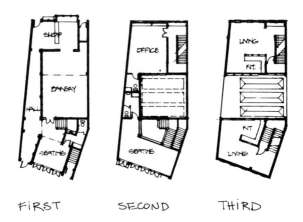

FIRST   SECOND   THIRD

Bakery north elevation and floor plans

46: HOUSING FOR THE ELDERLY

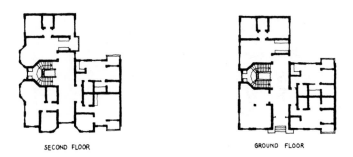

SECOND FLOOR   GROUND FLOOR

Housing for the elderly, northwest elevation and floor plans

47: ART GALLERY AND APARTMENTS

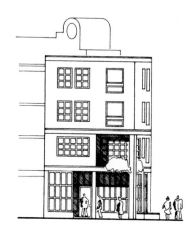

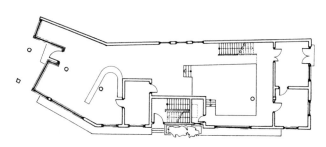

Elevation and art gallery plan

48: RESIDENCE

FIRST FLOOR

SECOND FLOOR

THIRD FLOOR

FOURTH FLOOR

Residence, north elevation and floor plans

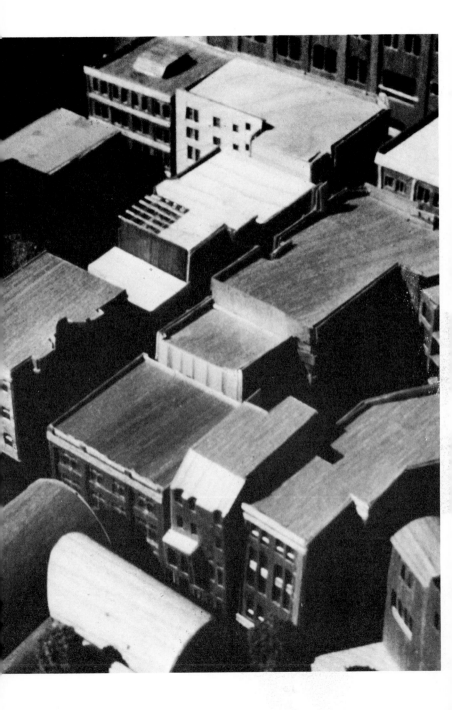

EXPERIMENT

Development on the south side of the main square continued now, as if to bridge the gap between the main square
and the newly formed ship repair terminal: a little spark,
in the form of a bandstand.

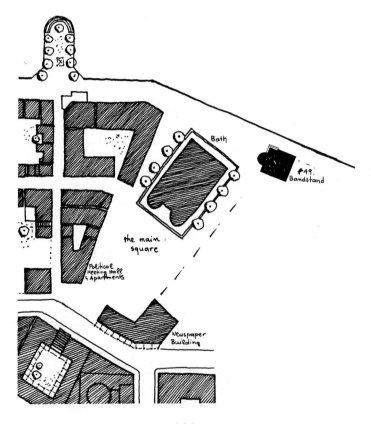

This was a true vision . . . something felt by Leslie Moldow, not expensive, but small, dramatic, and charming, a way of holding the corner of the square.

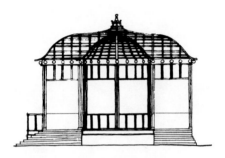

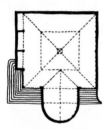

Bandstand elevation and plan

As soon as it had happened, it prompted a flurry of development beyond it.

50: PIER 24 PARK

Hajo Neis's words, written to the committee at that time:

Standing on the site in front of the water, behind the Bath,
on the main square, I imagine that I would like something
nice on pier 24 under the Bay Bridge, right opposite where

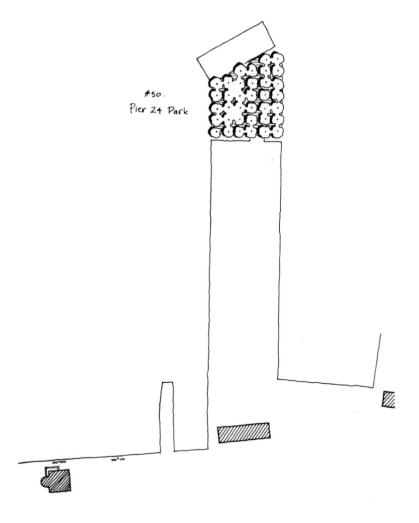

#50.
Pier 24 Park

EXPERIMENT

I am standing. The first thing which comes strongly to my mind is a grove of trees which pleases the eye, creating a place where one wants to go.

One can sit there, read the newspaper, make a drawing, play boule, or just walk around. People in our group told me that one of their favorite games in their childhood has been to play 'statues.' So I imagine all the 19 people of our group are playing statues under the trees.

Pier 24 park

EXPERIMENT

COMMENTARY

Development now continued on a wide variety of fronts: in the old grid, next to the main square, on the waterfront, near the freeway. . . .

We had reached a stage now, where most of the big structure had been created, or at least sketched out . . . and many of the projects did their best to enhance, develop, and fill in this structure.

Interesting individual projects done during this period included:

52: GYMNASIUM

53: PAVILION

54: SMALL PARK

57: MUSIC CONSERVATORY

58: PRIVATE RESIDENCE

The gymnasium, built as a publicly subsidized club by Hye Myoung Kim, next to the theater, gave the community athletic facilities.

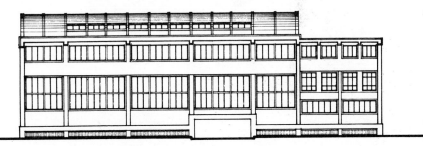

Gymnasium southwest elevation

EXPERIMENT

The pavilion, also proposed by Hye Myoung Kim, enhanced the structure of a small existing pier, not far from the main square . . . and made a further step in the development of interstitial structure between the main square and the south end.

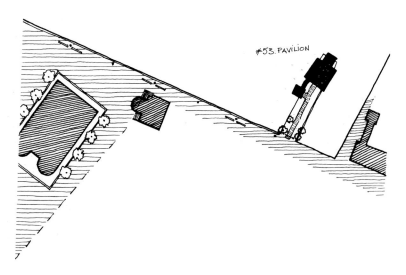

Pavilion east elevation and site plan

EXPERIMENT

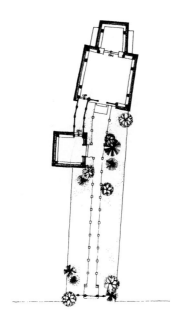

Plan and north elevation

The small park, with two rows of trees, enhances the axis of the pavilion.

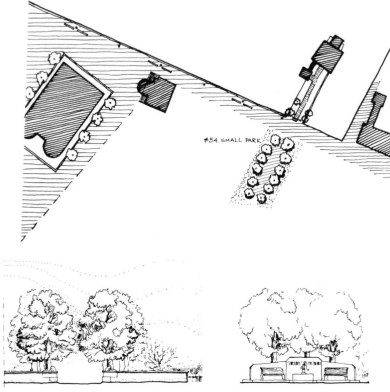

Small park, site plan and elevations

The music school helped to complete the backside of the grid.

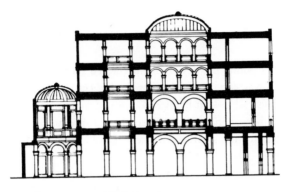

Music conservatory

And Hermann Diederich's private house, was one of the simplest and most charming buildings built within the grid itself.

FIRST FLOOR

SECOND FLOOR

THIRD FLOOR

Private house, street elevation and floor plans

EXPERIMENT

COMMENTARY ON THE FINAL STAGE

At this point, the development entered its final stage: one which was very interesting for the project.

Physically, what happened in this development was that a number of industrial and semi-industrial projects gathered to form a small square near the old piers and the Bay Bridge.

But what happened physically was, this time, only half the story. Even more significant, for the future of the theory of urban design which is described in this book, was the fact that the final stages of development which we shall describe now, were done almost entirely without the help of the committee.

So far, as we have explained, the projects were always done by a kind of cooperative process, back and forth between the committee and the members of the community . . . the committee indicating what needed to be done, and judging the proposals, the members of the community making the proposals and modifying them according to their visions.

What all this meant, effectively, was that the rules which were described in Part one, had not, up until now, been thoroughly understood by the members of the community. Although they were using the rules, the rules needed constant comment, explanation, clarification, and the members of the community were being educated constantly, as they used the rules: They made proposals, changed their proposals, watched them being built—and all the time, their grasp of the rules got better.

Warehouses, west elevation

Then, further back from the water, two very large projects were built:

60: COMMUNITY PARKING AND OFFICE BUILDING

61: CAR DEALERSHIP

Next, some subtle developments began to form a street between the main square and the warehouse area, also forming two intermediate centers on the way: a tiny square, and a small park near the pier, introduced earlier in the process:

63: LIBRARY

64: RESTAURANT AND LONG APARTMENT BUILDING

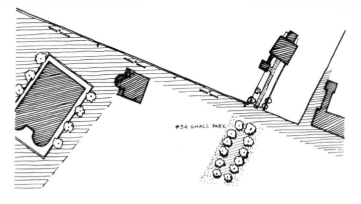

Existing situation, with small park introduced

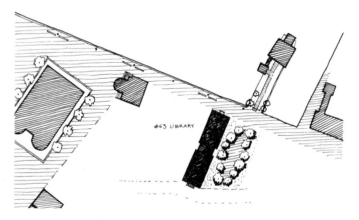

Step 1: Library defines the edge of the park

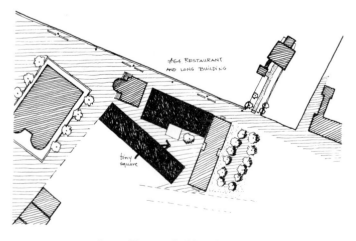

Step 2: Two new buildings form a tiny square

EXPERIMENT

FIRST FLOOR

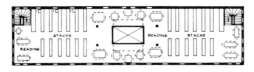

THIRD FLOOR

Library elevation, floor plans and section

Then, to seal the unclear space between the library with its park, and the warehouse area, Jim McLane proposed to build a furniture factory and Bruce Grulke an electronics factory. These factories, creating the small "working square," began the crystallization of the final phase. The factories required truck access, were near the warehouses, were close to the water, and stood at the end of a heavily truck-traveled street:

65: FURNITURE FACTORY

68: ELECTRONICS FACTORY

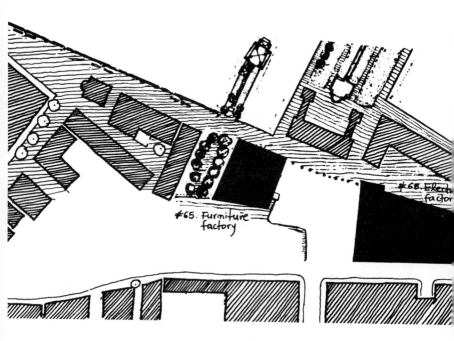

#65. Furniture factory

#68. Electronics factory

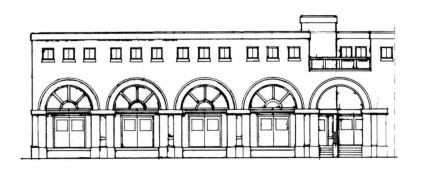

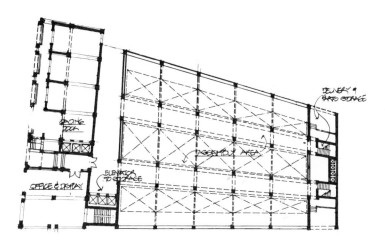

Electronics factory elevation and ground floor plan

Shortly afterward, two incremental details, which were to be added to the working square, began to give it a very definite character of its own:

71: BOLLARDS

72: PAVEMENT

The bollards set a boundary to the truck traffic, and also helped to make the square simultaneously industrial, and yet also pleasant and human . . . something rarely achieved in present-day cities.

Bollards on the square

And then the physical paving of the square, helped to intensify its character and orientation towards the water.

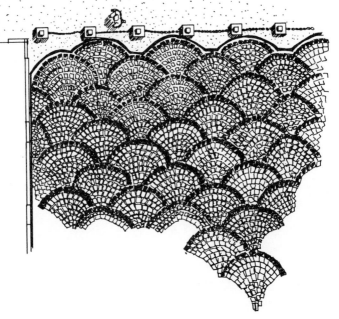

Pavement on the square

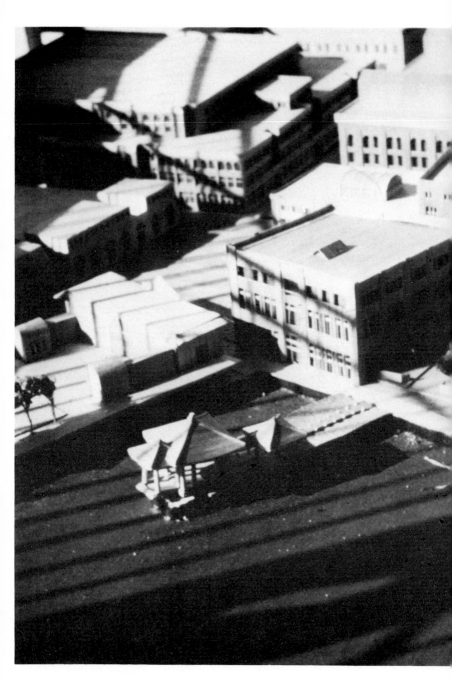

COMMENTARY

A few other finishing touches, large and small, completed the project, and filled in most of the gaps.

74: WALL

A wall built to enclose a playing area for teenagers, under the bridge, was simple and cheap. The playing area was described as having a dirt floor . . . "the ground of the field will get no special treatment . . . it is just a dirt patch enclosed by a wall."

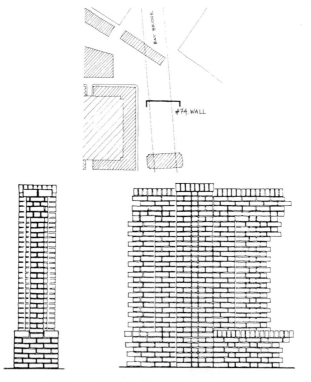

Wall site plan, section and elevation

80: HEALTH CLINIC

A rather large health clinic, near the main square, had the beautiful result of bridging the pedestrian street that goes south from the square, and thus brought the street to life:

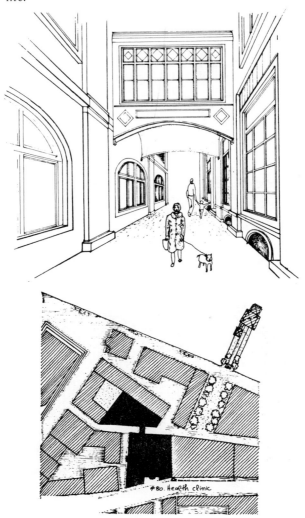

#80. Health clinic

EXPERIMENT

83: PAVING

Beautiful, carefully-made paving, which glistens when wet, completed the promenade, all along the waterfront.

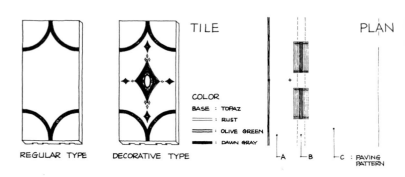

TILE

PLAN

COLOR
BASE : TOPAZ
———— : RUST
═══════ : OLIVE GREEN
━━━━━ : DAWN GRAY

REGULAR TYPE   DECORATIVE TYPE   └A   └B   └C : PAVING PATTERN

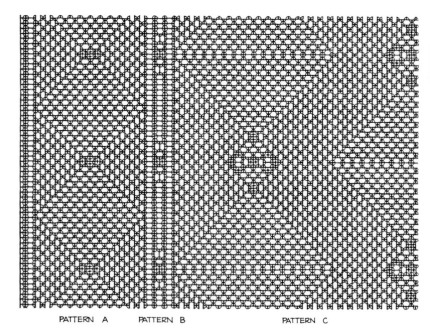

PATTERN A   PATTERN B   PATTERN C

84: A KIOSK

Between the theater, the conservatory, the newspaper building, and the political meeting hall, is a kiosk for announcements:

EXPERIMENT

88: FOUNTAIN

Artemis: "At the back side of the church, where the pedestrian path meets the promenade, a very small, intimate place between the church and the row of houses has already been created. I felt that something was needed there, that could bring people to that place. I imagined a small fountain against the back wall of the church, and a stone seat nearby, both of them under the shadow of a big olive tree."

Built with funds from public works:

PART THREE

EVALUATION

❧ ✤ ❧

All in all, we consider our experiment to be a success. It is successful enough, we believe, to indicate that the theory we have put forward is essentially correct.

On the other hand, there are also several problems and open questions, where a great deal of work remains to be done.

Let us first outline the successes.

Most obvious of all, the city which has been created, does have some of the positive character and structure we see in old cities. It does have the organic, personal, and human character which we associate with many of the most beautiful cities of the past, and which seems to be responsible for their success as environments. And it clearly does *not* have the obsessive, dead character of most "urban design" projects of recent decades.

In this sense we see the experiment as a success.

The project also has a nice, comfortable, informality. It is relaxed. There is an easy way in which the different projects fit together, and the wholeness which is produced, is produced in a nice, easy-going fashion.

In this sense, too, we may count it a success.

But the success is partial. First of all, the physical character of the city which has been created is more idiosyncratic than what we were aiming for. Its buildings are often not all as calm or unified as we had hoped.

Second, the large-scale structure is not as profound as we wanted it to be. Although the general disposition of the main square, mall, small grid, and so on, is quite nice, and is suitably informal . . . it does not yet have the profound unity of a place like Amsterdam or Venice. We do believe that the very high order of quality which we see in such cities, can ultimately be attained by means of a theory such as ours. But we have not attained it yet.

Third, the actual physical character of the buildings is rather weird. Our effort to make sure that the buildings contribute physically to the formation of unity, has produced—as a side effect—a very particular style which was not intended.

All in all, then, the unity of the project is not quite as deep as we had hoped. There is a partial unity. But the profound simplicity and unity which was often achieved in old towns, has not yet been achieved here.

In order to understand the reasons for this partial failure more fully, we shall now expand the discussion of the three problems just mentioned.

1. *The style of the buildings*

One might say, jokingly, that the theory apparently produces a late-nineteenth century pseudo-renaissance style of architecture. Even if we don't go this far, at the very least, we must admit that the physical style which appears throughout the projects, is slightly questionable.

We are fairly certain that this style came about mainly because our Rule 6, about construction, was not sufficiently well formulated. As a result, students were forced to rely on their perception of what we—the committee—considered "good construction." They were often naive about this, and unfortunately, we ourselves were not skilful enough to formulate Rule 6 in a way that would produce a more pure character. Also, we failed to see the rather strange direction of this "style," until it was too late to do anything about it.

While it is true that any correct formulation of the construction rule will tend to produce a more traditional appearance in the buildings—including more detail, window surrounds, cornices, bases, well-articulated columns, etc.— it is simply not true that it would need to produce the strange nineteenth-century character which we unintentionally produced. We consider the task of reformulating Rule 6, so that it can produce a more pure character, one of the first minor things which must be done to set the theory straight.

2. *Weakness of large-scale order*

Far more serious, as we have already mentioned, we feel that the project does not yet have a powerful enough sense of order at the largest scale.

A real field of centers is both more and less intense, both more and less differentiated; there is contrast between intensity and calmness. Some centers are unitary, like a main square or a gateway. Others are more diffuse, more a field-like repetition of smaller centers—like a street or a grid of streets.

It was difficult, within the rules of the experiment, for individual buildings to contribute to the larger centers in such a low-keyed way.

It seems that this happened because the idea of large wholes, expressed in Rule 2, is not yet powerful enough.

Let us consider, for example, the status of the main square.

If the theory were perfect, we believe that it would not only have produced a main square somewhere near the center, but would also have produced a field-like gradient, which could be felt throughout the project, in which every part of the project would "point" towards the main square. Thus, somehow, the whole project would have a physical structure showing a kind of centralized gradient, all of it sloping (metaphorically) towards the middle. This is, for example, what happens in Venice, where the main square is not just an isolated physical thing, but a part of a field effect where the structure and distribution of all the minor squares, islands, and bridges, somehow build up towards St. Mark's, to emphasize it and strengthen it.

If we had achieved something of this sort, one could then truly say that the main square was not merely a large physical object 400 feet long—but that it was the core of a much larger structure which embraces the whole physical extent of the project.

But we didn't achieve this with the square. And we didn't really achieve it with any of the other major wholes, either. Thus, unfortunately, even though we used Rule 2 with the intention of producing large-scale wholeness, we still created something which is too much an aggregate of parts, not a single, well-formed whole.

So far, we don't know how to modify Rule 2 so as to produce the single well-formed whole, instead of the aggregate of parts. However, it is certainly possible to imagine a version of Rule 2 which is more decisive, more aggressive, than the rule which we used.

For example, in our experiment, there was a tacit agreement, among the students and teachers, that we were trying to get large-scale order out of nothing. This kind of agreement could be expanded upon to form the basis of a stronger Rule 2, as it was in the case of the grid.

For the grid, the success came because the grid was specified as a general and *informal* understanding—not by means of a plan which was rigidly drawn or administered.

Thus, although the whole was given, and understood by each of the different players, still, the actual whole which emerged was flexibly and organically interpreted. Each person was still free to modify the whole, in such a way as to conform to the subtle details of his or her particular project. And the actual whole grew, not from the rigid explanation of a rule, but from the interpretation of the *idea* of this whole, by a variety of different people, with different private agendas.

Our success with the small grid of streets, leads us to believe that such methods could be expanded to become more successful. A similar, more widespread process, might be a success on a larger scale.

However, it would be essential to maintain a visionary character in the wholes . . . and not to allow any sort of rigid administration or master plan, to control the process. The exact form of rules which would allow this to be done, remains an open question.

3. *The road system*

By any standards, our treatment of vehicular roads must be considered unusual.

We have already explained, under section 4.4 of Rule

4, that we intentionally placed road traffic in an inferior position, which *followed* from the location of buildings and pedestrian space, instead of allowing roads to *generate* building form, as they usually do today.

We believe this principle is extremely important.

However, at the same time, the road system we created is informal to a degree—and might not work in a larger-scale project, where the connectivity of the streets, access, parking, and through traffic might play a more important role.

It is also important to add that in the actual experiment we did not use Rule 4.4 in its pure form, but supplemented it with certain informal understandings. For example, we shared an idea that the main road would be parallel to the water's edge, but some distance away from it, with pedestrian streets going down towards the water. We shared an idea that there would be no road along the water's edge, and that all parking would be in the "back" zone, away from the water. These informal understandings, similar to the holistic ideas proposed in the last section, for the creation of large-scale order, probably saved the rule . . . and in a real case would be essential.

It is clear that some modified and more sophisticated way of reformulating Rule 4.4 must be found, so that the road system becomes coherent, while still *following* the definition of buildings and pedestrian space.

∽ ✢ ∽

Let us now move on to a much more serious class of defects in our theory.

239

The problems we have discussed so far, are problems *within* the theory. They are problems largely caused by poor formulation of Rules 2, 4.4, and 6. There is every reason to believe that these problems can be solved by reformulating these rules. In this sense, there is no danger implied by these problems—that the basic theory *itself* might be faulty. These problems seem to leave the basic theory intact.

We come now to a class of *major* problems, which are not problems *inside* the theory, but problems *with* the theory. These are problems of implementation.

It is obvious that the theory we have presented says nothing, so far, about implementation.

In fact, the success of the theory, and of the experiment, depends on the fact that we intentionally ignored present rules of urban planning, zoning, urban administration, financing, and economics.

But, of course, in order for the theory to succeed, these problems must ultimately be dealt with.

And the trouble is, that the present methods of implementation are extremely different from the methods which would be required to implement this theory. The process we have outlined is incompatible with present-day city planning, zoning, urban real estate, urban economics, and urban law.

The fact that each project is guided by the emerging wholeness of the city, is a *really different idea* from current ideas about development.

It just isn't the same as zoning, which tries to impose fixed rules on development, without regard for the emerging whole. It just isn't the same as planning, which tries to create the whole by establishing plans, and then filling in slots. It just isn't compatible with urban real estate theory or bank lending policies, which define the highest and best use of a given piece of land according to the profit which can be derived from it.

The pure form of the process we have shown so far, is not even compatible with present forms of land ownership. The individual projects in our simulation were not guided or constrained by lot boundaries. Instead, each one took whatever space seemed needed to make the project whole. This could not happen if one paid attention to fixed lot lines, within the limits of present patterns and conceptions of ownership.

These major problems with the process we have defined, are of an entirely different order from the three problems we listed in the first section. They are different, above all, because we do not consider these matters to be *defects* in our process. *We list them as problems, because they require corrections in present society, and in existing planning law and planning process.*

Indeed, we consider that the present institutions, because they clearly are at odds with the process we have described, are highly problematic. The incompatibilities we have pointed to merely show in very graphic terms, how sadly and *drastically*, present-day methods, conceptions, and procedures are incompatible with the desire for wholeness. This is an indictment indeed. It is a very serious matter, of grave social concern. But of course, merely saying so does not solve the problem.

However, the task of reformulating urban processes of implementation, to make way for the kind of process we have defined, is an enormous one.

It is not enough to say that zoning, planning, economics, and land ownership, as they exist, are incompatible with what we have done. We need to show exactly how these four institutions might be changed, in a practical and feasible way, so that the kind of process we have defined really can be implemented on a large scale, in a city today.

So far we have not succeeded in doing this. We made some modest efforts, in a theoretical seminar given at the university at the same time that the project itself was going on. But we found that these matters could not be discussed with enough clarity in the purely theoretical atmosphere of the university.

This may be said to be the most serious defect in the theory we have presented. But of course, it is also its greatest strength, precisely because it shows that the theory is capable of stimulating an entirely new class of research and problem solving in the city.

In order to solve these problems, even to find preliminary answers, we believe that real-world experiments must be made, under conditions where city officials and other persons responsible for the implementation process, are committed to trying to work out methods by which all this can be done. Under these conditions, we believe the necessary reformulations and definitions will be found.

In conclusion, let us now go back and summarize the positive achievements of the theory. For this final discussion, we return, again, to the "one rule."

Up to a point, the seven rules which were given in Part one are adequate to produce the necessary urban structure. Operating, as they do, at a great variety of levels, both at different levels of scale, and at different levels of abstraction, they do, together, create a system of rules which is in principle almost enough to produce a healthy urban structure, by slow growth. They are reasonably precise: they are operational, and they are coherent.

But perhaps they are still not quite deep enough. They can produce an urban structure which is functionally sound, which is intact, which is coherent. But they will not, of themselves, produce a city which is moving, which has feeling in it, deep feeling, which is profound.

Of course it may be said that this profoundness cannot possibly itself be a product of any rules . . . but that it must, instead, simply be a product of the depth of spirit present in the makers, in the builders. And that when we feel this depth, this moving spirit, in some of the great cities of the past, we do so because these places were a product of men and women, who were themselves moved by deep spirit, and who therefore succeeded in allowing this deep spirit to reveal itself, in the places which they built.

Up to a point, this is certainly true. Depth of spirit cannot be "manufactured." And yet we believe that proper, and deep use of the one overriding rule itself *was* responsible for the spirit we observe in all great traditional towns.

This implies that the production of urban space must, in

the end, be based more on full understanding of the one rule, and less on the mechanical application of the seven temporary rules.

In order to have a sense of the direction in which this leads, we shall now make an effort to redefine the overriding rule, in a slightly more specific manner than we have done before.

Let us begin by looking back at the individual rules themselves. The rules vary. They deal with different topics: large topics, small topics, general topics, and very specific topics. They deal with parking, building shape, the position of columns in a building, the relation of a building to the urban space which is around it, the shape of a window, the position of a park or of a children's playground. In this sense they differ greatly.

But in another sense, the rules are immensely similar. All of them deal with wholes. Each one of the rules, which has been written down in Chapter three, and followed in our process, says, in one way or another, something about certain specific wholes in the city, how these wholes can be made more whole still, and how they must be related to still other wholes.

Note that, this insight tells us something we didn't know before.

We knew, from the beginning, that the one rule tells us to make the city whole, and that the specific rules tell us how to do it in detail.

What we shall now see is different. Each of the specific rules has told us how to do it, *by specifying a bunch, or cluster, of subsidiary wholes, and telling us how to form them, and how to make them whole.*

There is a play on words here which is not meant to be funny; it is important. (1) We have the meaning of the word "whole" as an entity, and (2) we have the meaning of the word "whole" as something healed.

It is the conjunction of these two meanings of the word whole which underlies all the rules which have been presented.

Each of the rules works by telling us to make certain definite entities or wholes (sense 1) more whole, more unified (sense 2). It always does this by telling us to insist on creating still other entities, within the whole. Thus the formation of entities, the formation of other wholes, makes the original wholes more whole.

To understand this clearly, let us consider each rule, one by one.

The principle is most clearly expressed in Rule 2, which quite deliberately emphasizes the fact that every act of building must play a role in helping to create larger urban structures in the city. That is, the rule says that each new whole which is a building project, must at the same time also help in the formation of certain larger wholes (the urban structures), which will be created gradually . . . by the accretion of individual acts. And, of course, the rule says that in fact, each act of building should participate in the creation of at least three different larger wholes: one which it helps to fill out, one which it helps to pin down, and one which it hints at . . . sets in motion. Thus, for Rule 2, it is rather obvious. But the same is true of all the other rules too.

If we examine the system of rules presented under Rule 4, the rules which govern the formation of urban space, we see the same general principle, working at a smaller scale. Here each rule is occupied with the formation of certain specific wholes, which contribute to parking, pedestrian movement, public open space, roads, indoor space, and building mass.

Thus for instance, Rule 4.1 explicitly requires that every building mass helps to create an identifiable, viable "chunk" of pedestrian space right next to it. Rule 4.5 says that whenever a shortage of parking reveals itself arithmetically, it is necessary to create a complete parking structure. Rule 4.5 also says that this parking structure may not be placed next to pedestrian space, thus protecting the wholeness of the pedestrian space, and another rule requires that parking structures be surrounded by other buildings whenever possible . . . thus reducing the negative impact of the parking structure on the larger area of space around it.

In general, these rules all define the way that the different wholes, which may exist at the level of public urban space, are interdependent, and must fit together in certain definite ways, to protect their mutual integrity.

If we look at the subrules of Rule 5, we see the same, at a still smaller scale. Here we have rules describing the way that the masses of a building (its subsidiary wholes) are related to the main mass (the main whole), the way that the entities or wholes defined by main entrances are to be clearly visible to a person entering, the way that arcades or passages or courtyards of circulation are to exist within the building in order to clarify its larger wholeness by means of the disposition of its smaller wholes . . . even, in the last few subrules of the chapter (5.21–5.25) the way that individual rooms, offices, and waiting areas are to be shaped and placed together, to guarantee their individual and collective wholeness.

In Rule 6, we see the same concerns, now at still smaller levels of scale, this time concerning themselves with structural bays, columns, beams, the base of the building, the shape of the windows, the top of the building, and the shape of individual columns, capitals, and window panes.

In Rule 1, which deals with the most basic aspects of piecemeal growth, we see the same again, albeit in more elementary fashion. We see here explicit statements about the way that the larger whole (of the entire area), must be built up from small wholes, with the statistical distribution of these smaller wholes given by size and function.

Even in Rule 3, perhaps the most enigmatic, which deals with visions, we see again the same, expressed in the fact that the functional vision which precedes any given building project, must essentially develop the proposed project—as something which clearly heals, or "springs" from the surrounding structure . . . and embellishes it, enlarges it, extends it, and completes it.

Finally, Rule 7 adds an insight of another sort altogether. We stated in Part one, that wholeness is composed of a field of "centers," and that wholes must ultimately be understood as centers. Rule 7 specifies the geometry of a center in a rudimentary way, which helps in the geometrical formation of each whole. Once again, essential to this geometrical idea, is the fact that the wholeness, or "healed-

247

ness," of a given whole relies on the extent to which this whole is successfully composed of other wholes, without gaps between them.

This is the theme throughout the details of the seven rules. All the different rules in Chapter three are all aimed at trying to produce a larger wholeness, by creating intermediate and smaller wholes, and by means of the different and specific relationships between the smaller wholes at different levels.

This tells us something new and definite about the one rule, which we did not know before.

To make it clear, we may reformulate the one rule abstractly in the following basic way: *Every building increment must be chosen, placed, planned, formed, and given its details in such a way as to increase the number of wholes which exist in space.*

Although this is still by no means the full story about the one rule, it does bring us a great deal closer to proper understanding of the way the rule works.

When the rule is followed in this form, there is the beginning of a reasonable guarantee that space will become more whole, and that the city will then gradually be healed.

From an empirical point of view, what may we conclude?

We have found that a process which is motivated and guided entirely by the search for wholeness, produces an entirely different effect from current practice in urban design, and goes far to remedy the defects which cities have today.

The central thought behind our work, is that an urban process can only generate wholeness, when the structure of the city comes from the individual building projects and the life they contain, rather than being imposed from above. Wholeness only occurs when the larger urban structure, and its communal spaces, spring from these individual projects.

We have found that the detailed rules necessary to generate this wholeness in an urban development process, can be formulated in a precise and operational fashion that can be easily understood and used.

And we believe that the overall approach that we have presented, provides an entirely new theoretical framework for the discussion of urban problems. It can be regarded as the beginning of a new theory which is strong enough to allow open questions and unsolved problems to be solved in a fruitful way.

ACKNOWLEDGMENTS

This experiment would have been impossible without the cooperation of faculty and students from the University of California. We thank all the following students whose work appears together with that of Hajo Neis and Artemis Anninou in the foregoing pages.

Colette Cage
Shohreh Daemi
Hermann Diederich
Hubert Froyen
Bruce Grulke
Ramzi Kawar
Hye Myoung Kim
Takeshi Kimura
James McLane
Leslie Moldow
Mahn Oh
Carsten Schmunk
Alice Sung
Martine Weissmann

These students worked very very hard, and far beyond the call of duty, to build the beautiful model shown in the photographs and to complete all their drawings of the projects.

We also thank Howard Davis for his very helpful contribution to the project as a part-time lecturer.

And we thank Marian Wattman for her tireless work in editing and bringing the manuscript to completion.